World Famous

How to Give Your Business a Kick-Ass Brand Identity

David Tyreman

American Management Association

New York • Atlanta • Brussels • Chicago • Mexico City • San Francisco
Shanghai • Tokyo • Toronto • Washington, D.C.

This publication is designed to provide accurate and authoritative
information in regard to the subject matter covered. It is sold with
the understanding that the publisher is not engaged in rendering
legal, accounting, or other professional service. If legal advice or
other expert assistance is required, the services of a competent
professional person should be sought.

Library of Congress Cataloging-in-Publication Data

Tyreman, David.
    World famous : how to give your business a kickass brand
identity / David Tyreman.—1st ed.
        p.   cm.
    Includes index.
    ISBN-13: 978-0-8144-0934-3
    ISBN-10: 0-8144-0934-2
    1. Target marketing.   2. Branding (Marketing)   I. Title.
HF5415.127.T87   2009
658.8'27—dc22

                                                    2009006298

Printing number

10   9   8   7   6   5   4   3   2   1

For my partner in crime, Theo Garcia:

Thank you for telling me "yes you can" when my pen said "no you can't." I love you more than words can say.

For my parents, Jean and John Tyreman:

Thank you for embracing my journey, even when you didn't know what on earth I was talking about. I love you.

Contents

Contents

Contents

STEP 5: READY, SET, ENGAGE!   171

Preface

There are masses of people just waiting to do business
with you once they are so inspired.

I hope you stop right now and write that down. Post it on your computer, on your bathroom mirror, and in your car. Make it your screen saver, print a poster-sized version of it, or even embroider it on a pillow. I want you to place this truth where you can see it several times a day, every day, because it will serve as a reminder of what is possible if you simply work to *inspire* rather than sell, to be *authentic* rather than try to fit in, and to *engage* your marketplace rather than focus solely on your competitors.

The fact that there are masses of people waiting to be inspired by you is absolutely fantastic news, because it means that the power is in your hands. You can do inspiration. It's much easier than trying to keep up with "the other guy." And it's much more fun.

You are about to embark on a life-changing journey toward building a World Famous brand identity. Along the way, you may get lost and feel confused. You may want to give up and go back to business as usual. There will be times when you think you don't know anything at all, when you feel silly, or brain-dead, or boring, or dumb. It happens to all of us, and posting the quote can help you out of that slump. I've yet to meet anyone who was not relieved and renewed after reading (and remembering) that masses of people are poised and ready to do business with him once they are so inspired.

We've all had days when we feel that success is out of our reach, when we are convinced that we don't have what it takes to realize our dreams. I call them "lottery days," when we feel that success is all about luck and we missed school the day they were passing it out. When you wake up on a lottery day and can't shake that loser feeling, just read the quote. It's absolutely true—there really and truly are masses, *masses* of people waiting for *you* to inspire them. They want it. They need it. And you are the perfect person to give it to them.

Ready for some more good news? A vast marketplace is poised and ready to sign up with your company for a lifetime. That's right, a lifetime. Not because you are a great salesperson, not because your company has a winning ad campaign, but because your brand identity resonates with these people on a deeply personal level. You inspire raving, lifelong fans when you create a brand identity that has an authentic personality and a vibrant attitude that people can relate to, a brand identity that provides consumers with experiences they want and even need to have, and that elicits feelings they yearn to feel.

When you touch people's hearts and minds, they are compelled to do business with you. They form a relationship with you, they feel they know you like a friend, and they see you as a natural fit for the story of their life. Cultivate a brand following by providing a meaningful experience that resonates with people. Do this consistently, and you will inspire a loyalty to your brand that cannot be swayed. Do this with authenticity, and your brand will become World Famous.

Business is not just a transaction; it's an experience. People do more business with people and companies that engage them in the purchasing experience. When you attach meaning to the act of doing business with you, you stand out from the crowd.

Think of all the businesses you have visited and never returned to, despite your having no real complaint with them. You might even have completely forgotten about many of the businesses you once used. You may have purchased real estate, airline tickets, insurance, haircuts, sandwiches, or clothing and forgotten all about the business you used. These forgettable businesses do not have an effective brand identity. They are simply providing a function. They work hard, they do a perfectly fine job, but they are not connecting with you in a way that means something, in a way that stimulates you in any particular way.

Think of the meaning, the feeling attached to owning a Rolls-Royce, watching a James Bond movie, or drinking a Coke. What does it *mean* to be a consumer of these products? What about the products and services you prefer? Are you an Apple or a PC person? Do you drive "American"? Are you a Letterman or a Leno fan? I would bet you were able to answer these questions without hesitation. Why? Because whatever your answers were, they hold meaning for you; they fit in with the story of your life. The brands you choose are your personal statement about who you are, and so it is with your marketplace.

Which big, well-known companies inspire your loyalty? Perhaps there's an airline, an automobile manufacturer, or a bookstore chain. You feel a special chemistry with that company, a desire to repeat the experience of choosing its brand. The enjoyment of "belonging" to the brand, of being the type of person who uses its products exclusively keeps you coming back for more. Even the giants of industry can compel your tunnel vision, so that you are blind to the competition.

Being World Famous is about more than being well known. A World Famous brand is one that people feel a real affinity with, one that they love to visit and talk about. World Famous brands know who they are and stay true to their unique vision, which inspires confidence in consumers. It's no shock that the truly World Famous brands are also the great success stories, backed up by legions of loyal fans and healthy profits.

Any business can be World Famous—including yours. A little hole-in-the-wall dry cleaner has the capacity to engage its market in such a way that customers will travel all the way across town—twice—just to have their clothing cleaned by that particular company.

You have your own list of companies that hold a special place in your heart, companies that you simply love to do business with. That favorite coffee shop, the father-and-son team that cleans your carpets, the restaurant that feels like a home away from home. You may not even be able to put your finger on what it is that compels you to go back again and again, but you know that your favorite companies will always be the only choice in your heart and mind. You can become the only choice in your marketplace, too, by daring to stand out and differentiate your brand.

I started my company in my garage and nurtured my brand until it became World Famous within my market. So did Amazon. com. And FedEx. And countless other World Famous brands that you use or hear about every single day. If they can do it, if I can do it, you can too.

What began as an idea about how to sell antiques in a unique way evolved into a multimillion-dollar visual branding company, which led me to my true calling: helping individuals and businesses develop a kick-ass brand identity. My passion went beyond selling visual merchandise, and so after selling my share of the company I cofounded, I started over again with a mission to make the essential components of successful branding accessible to people like you.

In the 20 years I have been in the United States, I have worked with thousands of businesses, many of them World Famous. I have worked with international branding companies, small businesses, and independent professionals—everyone from attorneys to Zen practitioners to La-Z-Boy sales hopefuls, from upstarts to giants like Levi's, Nike, and Old Navy.

It's funny how many times I have seen people scratch their heads, wondering how "they" do it, when the secrets of brand success are right there out front for everyone to see, like neon signs beaming messages into the night sky. There are basic fundamentals that every person can learn to help build a World Famous brand identity, and this book will help you master them.

The process is surprisingly simple and loads of fun. As you work the five steps to building a World Famous brand identity, I will challenge you to dig deep and find your authentic voice, to shed your fears and dare to stand out in the crowd. You will find your own superniche marketplace and learn exactly what motivates the people in it to do business with you. With your focus honed like a laser beam, you will discover the insider secrets of brand differentiation, develop a three-word persona, invite your superniche into the vicarious playground that is your brand, and learn the importance of firmly committing to the promise of your brand.

By turning your negative experiences into unique offerings, you will add value to your brand, cementing your position in the marketplace as the obvious choice. In the final step, you will be given specific tools to help you engage the marketplace, uncovering all of the ways in which your business touches the world and how you can use each of these aspects of your business to cultivate a World Famous brand. By the end of the book, you will have a brand profile in hand similar to the profiles I create for my world-class clients, a tool that is powerful enough to catapult your business to World Famous status.

World Famous is about building a pipeline between your market and your bank account. It's for entrepreneurs, would-be entrepreneurs, and those of you who want to make your mark on the world. World Famous is for those who want to grow their business in unique, daring, and authentic ways. It's for mavericks, trailblazers, visionaries, and nonconformists. It's for the next Richard Branson, Steve Jobs, and Ralph Lauren, the next Martha Stewart, Vera Wang, and Oprah Winfrey.

The process you are now engaged in is primarily about thinking differently, approaching everyday situations from a new perspective. The following pages will challenge your preconceived notions about business. Conventional wisdom will take a backseat to innovation as you break through limiting thoughts to find the brilliance that is your unique brand identity.

As you read this book, you will find that you get more excited about your business. You will come up with new ideas as you start recognizing the opportunities around you. You will learn how to add life to your organization, generating passion not just from your business but also toward your business *from* your marketplace. And you will learn how to cultivate a consumer base that lives vicariously through your brand, so that doing business with your company holds a place of significance similar to the way a person feels when she receives not just a ring, but a ring from Tiffany; not just a car, but an Aston Martin; not just an award, but an Oscar.

Your business can hold that same significance for your marketplace. Your brand can be World Famous. Why take the time to work on your business if you are willing to settle for less? Why even start a business or join a company unless your goal is to make it stand out as the essential, absolute, earth-shattering obvious choice in people's hearts and minds? Why bother putting energy and effort into building your company unless it is going to stand out so brilliantly that it is, in fact, World Famous?

Will your company rise to the heights of Starbucks, Apple, or Amazon.com? That's entirely up to you. It certainly can. This journey into building a World Famous brand identity works for every type of business, not just those that are fortunate enough to have knockout new products *and* a few billion set aside for marketing.

This process works even if you have only the five dollars you just found down the back of the sofa. It works even if the product or service you offer is exactly the same as the one offered by the guy next door, the guy down the street, and the guy around the corner. Because ultimately, the secret to making your business World Famous is not really locked up in your product or service; it's all about how you make people feel and think about your brand. The secret to your success, to your World Famous brand identity, rests wholly in the hearts and minds of your marketplace.

This book is your all-access pass to the world of World Famous brand identity, a step-by-step approach that, when followed, will ensure that your business stands out as the obvious choice. Your brand identity is the most important asset you have. This book will help you build your own truly authentic brand identity. It's not about gimmicks, and it's not about tricks. Your company must *mean* something to your intended marketplace. I will help you find the meaning, inspiring masses of people to literally line up to do business with you.

You are about to embark on an adventure, one that shows you how to create a World Famous brand identity. Are you ready?

World Famous

The Obvious Choice

"Success isn't about being perceived as the best at what you do, it's about being perceived as the only one who does what you do."

—JERRY GARCIA OF THE GRATEFUL DEAD

If I asked you, "Do you want your business to be World Famous?" you would probably say something like, "Hello! I bought the book. Of course I want my business to be World Famous!"

I frequently speak in front of one thousand or more entrepreneurs, and all of them answer, "Yes!" when I ask that question. But that resounding affirmation is usually followed by the following statements:

"I want to be the best!"
"I want to be number one!"
"I want to beat out my competition!"

In all my travels and all my years of business, being "number one" has been the primary goal of the majority of the people I meet. At one time, it was my goal, too—until I learned that there is something better than being number one. That's right; there is a higher goal, a more rewarding goal, a goal that can be the difference between mediocrity and brilliance, between pennies and millions.

1

That goal is simply to stand out as the obvious choice, the *only* choice in the hearts and minds of your market.

The very concept of "being number one" is flawed because it suggests that there are other choices, that you are part of a group. It sets you up for comparison. Worse, it suggests that there is a war on and that only one company can win. Buying into the belief that there can be only one winner in your war of the brands takes your focus away from the unique identity of your business.

Not only is standing out as the obvious choice far superior to the objective of "being number one," but it is also safer. The great risk of trying to be "the best" is that you start looking closely at what your competitors are doing instead of looking at what your marketplace might want, instead of innovating. Rather than lead, you can accidentally succumb to one of the biggest invisible mistakes in business: comparing your business to other businesses that you deem "successful" and inadvertently emulating them.

As you jockey for the top position, you implement strategies and ideas that are based on what your competitors are doing. If they offer six, you offer seven. If they slash prices, you follow suit. Yet the more you emulate your competitors, the more similar you and they become, and this ultimately leads to your company becoming totally invisible. Eventually, your brand looks so much like the "other guy" that consumers have a hard time telling you apart. Homogeneous brands never rise above; they simply stay in the trenches fighting it out while distinctive, authentic brands cause a sensation in the marketplace.

Trying to one-up the competition has nothing—*nothing* —to do with your marketplace. Consumers are not interested in your fight to be number one. They want you to make them feel special. They want you to speak to them, to make them feel important and unique when they choose to do business with you. In essence, they want your brand to be about them, not about the competition. When you focus your attention on being number one, you take your attention *away* from your consumer. Why would anyone want to do business with a company that ignores his desires?

I'm not suggesting that you ignore your competitors completely—you certainly must keep abreast of the competition if you are to achieve success. What I am saying is that you mustn't get sucked into silly fights or, even worse, risk becoming a commodity, where your business is so similar to those of the other players in the market that the market dictates the price you can charge. You must stay true to who you are, and you must stay true to your marketplace.

In this book, I'm using two stellar, World Famous brands as examples as you build your brand profile. One is Polo Ralph Lauren, a former client of mine, and the other is Virgin Atlantic, a hugely successful airline owned by the infamous Richard Branson, founder of Virgin Records. The reason Virgin Atlantic wins so many industry awards is that it is truly an example of the number one (*and only*) rule for standing out from the crowd: Don't become part of the crowd in the first place. It's such an important rule, let's repeat it and write it down: The one and only rule to remember when you are seeking to stand out from the crowd is: *Don't become part of the crowd in the first place.*

Virgin Atlantic routinely wins awards for "Best in Class," and one of the ways it has been able to achieve this is by *creating its own class.* Virgin does not have a first-class section or a business-class section—it has Upper Class, which is positioned to beat out any other airline's business-class service, and Premium Economy, which is positioned to beat out any other airline's economy class. Virgin Atlantic doesn't compete on the same level as other airlines, yet it still wins award after award.

Do you see how Virgin Atlantic carved its own path and *defined* its own brand rather than let the industry norms dictate to its brand? Virgin also created its own language, "Upper Class," which differentiated the brand from other airlines. If you want to fly Upper Class, there's only one airline that can give you that experience, and that's Virgin.

(Actually, Richard Branson wanted to call his economy class the "Riff-Raff" section, but his investors balked at the idea. It's too bad, because I would have loved to fly "Riff-Raff," and there's no doubt that it would have been a huge hit.)

So while other airlines duke it out, trying to one-up each other with inches of leg room and special offers, Richard Branson is inspiring his marketplace to view Virgin Atlantic as the only choice. One airline might win out this week and another the next, but these airlines will never inspire brand loyalty the way Virgin does because people don't feel connected to their brand. Virgin Atlantic has a well-defined brand identity; the company has a distinct personality, attitude, and values that cause people to feel connected to it in a specific way.

When you focus on standing out as the obvious choice, your approach moves away from self-centric strategies toward developing a relationship with your marketplace. And when you connect with your market on an emotional level, people feel compelled to do business with you.

Look, there are dozens of ways to measure who is top gun: sales, market share, customer satisfaction, and on and on. Being number one is therefore a vague idea, one that you could go crazy trying to achieve. So do you want your business to be number one in some arbitrary category, or do you want masses of people to be *compelled* to do business with you because you are the obvious choice?

Webster's Revised Unabridged Dictionary defines *compel* as "to drive or urge with force, or irresistibility." Irresistibility. Wouldn't you love to be irresistible to your marketplace? Now *that's* a goal worth striving for. To illustrate the power of this objective, let me explain why I am personally compelled to do business with Virgin Atlantic.

On a cold day in January many years ago, I somehow talked my way into a free upgrade to Upper Class on Virgin Atlantic. Feeling rather full of myself, I told a tall tale about my "best friend Richard Branson," which got the attention of a gate manager named Ray. It was all in good fun, and everyone was in on the joke. Still, I was somewhat surprised when Ray came through with the free upgrade.

I still remember what it felt like to walk into the Upper Class cabin that day. I was overcome with the feeling that I had arrived, that I was home. I was so exhilarated that I thought I might explode with giddy laughter. The vibrant colors, the massive seats, the modern bar, the three-tier cake stand filled with treats, the personal entertainment system, the goodie bag with my own sweatsuit, socks, travel toiletries, and eyeshades—it all felt as though it were rightfully mine. I knew I would never be the same.

Once we were airborne, Ray was at my side, asking if everything was to my liking. I thanked him profusely and asked for his card. Later, I sipped champagne, enjoyed the all-day-all-night menu, and indulged in a manicure and a neck and shoulder massage. I sat at the bar hobnobbing with other passengers, laughed and joked with the very attractive and helpful flight crew, and lapped up every single second of the experience.

I was hooked. It was so exciting to be part of that world. It wasn't snooty or stuffy; it was hip and stylish. Far from business as usual, the crew made us feel as though this was their most important flight and we were their most important passengers. I felt as though Virgin had read my mind and discovered my deepest desires and personal tastes. From the menu choices to the décor, everything fit me to a tee. This was no one-time piece of luck, not a "so this is how the other half lives" sort of experience. This was my glimpse into the future—my future.

Back home in San Francisco, I could not shut up about my experience. I doubt that there was a person within five miles of me who didn't hear about my experience with Virgin Atlantic. I sent Ray a thank-you card and a very nice gift, and he responded with a handwritten thank-you note and made a point of letting me know that I should contact him whenever I was flying from London's Heathrow Airport. He also let me know about a friend who could do the same for me Stateside, a gate manager named Chris. I was in!

For the next five years, I enjoyed the absolute unbridled pleasure of flying in Virgin Atlantic's Upper Class cabin both to and from London. I would simply purchase the cheapest ticket I could find and then call Chris and Ray to make sure they would be working on my travel dates. I got very used to my awesome home in the sky. In fact, I started to take it for granted. Until, that is, one fateful day when Chris was not at the check-in as promised.

Unable to convince the Cruella De Vil clone in Chris's place that I should be in Upper Class, I asked how much it would cost to pay for the upgrade. "That will be $9,000, *sir*," she informed me with her right eyebrow raised as if to say, "Gotcha." Needless to say, I ended up in economy. I spent the entire flight wedged in between two passengers, catching the odd glimpse into Upper Class. It was the longest flight of my life. And it was the very last time I ever purchased an economy ticket on Virgin Atlantic.

From that day forward, I found a way to pay for the Upper Class experience. I was happy to scrape together the cash to buy the Upper Class ticket. It made me feel legitimate, like I had really earned it. The Upper Class experience on Virgin Atlantic speaks to the story of my life. It makes sense to me; it's as if it has my name written all over it. For me, there is only one choice. I must fly Virgin. And I must have a seat in Upper Class.

In a world of options, Virgin Atlantic stands out as the obvious choice, the only choice for me. I have an emotional connection to this company; I feel that I have a relationship with it. My heart and mind are engaged in the idea of flying with it. I am compelled to do business with Virgin Atlantic.

Overwhelmed with choices, people are in search of a brand experience they can identify with, a brand that fits into the story of their lives. Your marketplace doesn't really care if your company is number one if people aren't made to feel great about it; they want to feel that your brand is part of *who they are*. Your marketplace is waiting for you to distinguish your business as the obvious choice—the only choice.

Effective branding is not a mystery that only a chosen few will solve. It is not reserved for celebrities, giant corporations, or the wealthy. Anyone, and by anyone I mean *even you*, can create an effective brand identity that compels people to do business with her. You will pull this off. You will amaze your customers and your colleagues. Most of all, you will amaze yourself. And you will do it by engaging in a process of discovery, by following the five steps to creating a kick-ass brand identity:

Step 1: *Dare!* Dare to be different, to stand out from the crowd, to create a brand identity that is authentic and meaningful.

Step 2: *Discover the power of the superniche.* Learn why people buy, what inspires brand loyalty, and get to know your target market in a powerful way.

Step 3: *A defined differentiation.* Determine the three essential words that encapsulate your brand identity, and discover the playground and the promise of your brand.

Step 4: *Adding value.* Transform problems into opportunities to add value to your brand.

Step 5: *Ready, set, engage!* Use your new brand identity to connect with your marketplace.

Let's get started!

Dare!

Dare!

What is your biggest fear in business, or in life? For me, it was being poor, which was how I measured failure. To be poor was to fail. So, imagine my horror when I discovered that I was absolutely and completely flat broke! I hadn't a penny to my name. Not one cent. I also had something worse than bad credit: I had no credit—no credit cards, no overdraft protection, and no friendly bank manager who was willing to give me a line of credit or emergency funds. When I say I was broke, I mean I was *broke*!

How did I get that way? My adventure started with a fantastic idea I had: selling English antiques and vintage items to Americans using the same method that was used to sell Tupperware. I would throw "Antique Parties" in people's homes! I even had a fancy name for my new company: The London Antique Emporium. It was a sure thing . . . or so I thought.

Before leaving England, I excitedly shared my idea with everyone I knew, and every one of them told me that my idea was dumb. Even my boss in London told me, "You'll come crawling back, you loser." Nice send-off, don't you think? Despite the lack of support, I stuck to my guns and followed through with my plan.

My business partner and I arrived in the States in August of 1988 with a suitcase, a dream, and $5,000. We got busy right away, convincing friends and neighbors to host parties for us. We knew from the first party that something wasn't right, but we pressed on. After one too many lousy parties, we realized that my idea was not going to work. There I was, just a few short months after launching my business, and I was moments away from proving my boss, and everyone else back in England, right. I was despondent. Very shortly after, I was broke.

On a Tuesday in late October, my business partner and I sat at the kitchen table in our rented apartment, staring at our last $20 bill. "Any ideas?" he asked. A typical Englishman, I had the bright idea of spending our last $20 at the local pub. I knew the pub in Huntington Beach had a special on Tuesday nights: all the beer you could drink for $7, and unlimited nachos for $2.99. We could afford one last night out. As they say in England, one for the road!

It was a night I will never forget. Despite our circumstances, we had the time of our lives. We made friends with the bar staff and other patrons, and we told the story of our demise. When people heard that we were spending our last $20, they bought us drinks and asked us to talk about our adventure. We shared it all—the highs, the lows, the missteps, and the tiny successes. People hugged us.

Our new friends told us how inspired they were by our story, and how exciting our lives were compared to their own. To top it all off, one of the patrons owned a limousine company, and so he drove us home in style. So far being broke wasn't half bad, but as we rode home, I knew that my day of reckoning was but a few hours away.

As I glided into consciousness the next day, I realized that it had finally happened. I was penniless. I had dreaded this day all my life, and here it was. But wait! I was still breathing. I was alive. The world had not come to an end.

Despite the hangover, despite the brutal financial reality, I actually felt relief. I no longer had to worry about going broke—I was already there! I also felt something amazing, something that I had thought I said good-bye to along with our last $20: I felt hope. With nothing to lose, I realized that I had everything to gain, and with that realization, I found that I had a new sense of commitment to my goal. I had tied my hopes to money, believing that without money, I was hopeless. But it wasn't true. I had lived through my worst nightmare, and it really wasn't that bad.

Enormously relieved, I realized something that I had not understood until that very morning: Giving up was not an option. I had no idea how I would make it work, but right then and there, I vowed to make our business a success. I had failed miserably, and the experience was liberating. Without the fear of failure, I could do anything. After all, the worst thing that could happen was that I would fail again, and I already knew firsthand that I would survive it. In fact, my night out on the town as a total failure was the best night of my life.

I dared myself to make a go of it, no matter what. And you know what? I did. In just seven years, I went from having a zero net worth to being a multimillionaire. We had formed a new company, Propaganda, and acquired prestigious clients like Guess, Levi's, Macy's, Nike, Nordstrom's, Old Navy, and Polo Ralph Lauren, among others, and we had cultivated a media presence. Because of the way we approached business and our success in the market-place, we were featured on more than 100 television programs on networks like CNN and Fox; we even made the front page of the *Wall Street Journal.* We dared to rise above our failure. It was a huge dare, and it made us World Famous.

Why do I love to tell this story? Because I'm a show-off, of course. Seriously, though, it's a story that perfectly demonstrates what can happen when you dare yourself to make it. Remember, I had to make that dare twice: first when I came to the States suitcase in hand, and then again after I had failed. Once I saw the benefit of a daring attitude toward life and business, I never stopped daring. My road to success was paved with hundreds of dares. Daring my-self, my staff, and even my clients made me who I am today.

Dare to dare yourself.

Dare to go forward despite your fear of failure.

Dare to get creative when challenged.

Dare to try, try again; to push on; to persevere.

Dare to hold fast to your dreams, no matter what.

CHAPTER 1

Dare to Stand Up and Be Counted

Does your fear of speaking up date back to history class, when you were afraid to raise your hand even though you knew the answer? Maybe you're not afraid to speak your mind, but are you jumping on every fantastic opportunity that comes your way? Or are you nervous that you'll stand out *too much*? Or are you daring enough, but you still find that you're emulating those around you, simply by accident?

World Famous is not—I repeat, *not*—about being perfect, acceptable, and squeaky-clean. Being World Famous is about positioning yourself for success. In business, we are presented with numerous opportunities to succeed and grow. We learn from going for it every time, even if we make mistakes. With the sweat rolling down our backs and our stomachs churning, we push past our fears and dare to stand up and be counted. *That* is World Famous.

So how did my business partner and I go from broke to rolling in it in just seven years? Of course it takes more than one truth, more than one dare, and more than one revelation to build a World Famous business. But there was a defining moment that changed our course forever, the moment I learned that I could play with the big guys if I was willing to stand up and be counted. If I *believed* I could do it and acted on that belief, then I would do it.

It wasn't long after that fateful night when we spent our last $20 that I realized that as antique dealers, we had tons of competition. Looking under "Antiques" in the Yellow Pages, I found page after page of antique dealers, antique emporiums, antique malls, antique stores, and antique warehouses. How on earth could we ever compete with all of these varied and established businesses?

I started to feel worse when I visited some of our competitors and noticed the type of cars antique dealers drove. They were no better than the heap of junk I was driving, which had more duct tape than vinyl on the seats and more smoke than a David Copperfield show. Here I was aspiring to have a business that would clearly not make much money. Yet my garage had a few thousand dollars' worth of merchandise stored in it, and then there were the hunger pangs in my belly (the great motivator)!

There had to be a way to approach selling antiques that would generate a reasonable, if not sizable, amount of cash. I started wandering around shopping malls looking for inspiration (and a cheap lunch). I noticed that quite a few stores used antique and vintage items in their window and in-store displays. So I made a list of the stores that might want our antiques and started my sales calls.

Did we get a sale? Of course not. No one wanted to buy. They either had just placed an order, had no budget, or could buy only from companies on their approved list of vendors. We were rejected over and over again, and still I persisted. Sure, we made the odd sale here and there, enough to keep us in socks and beer, but we were barely getting by.

We figured out pretty quickly who our main competition was. Every time a store had "just placed an order," it was with this company. I'll call it Vintage, Inc. It wasn't that we were being rejected on our merits; another company had most of the business sewn up. Everywhere I turned, there it was: Vintage, Inc., . . . Vintage, Inc., . . . Vintage, Inc. Who were these guys, and how did they corner my market?

When I found out what we were up against, my heart sank.

Based on the East Coast, Vintage, Inc., had a 50,000-square-foot warehouse, $10 million in inventory, and salespeople all over the country looking after its customers. We had a 400-square-foot garage, $3,000 in inventory, and two blokes from England.

The more I learned about Vintage, Inc., the more I realized that even *I* wouldn't do business with me. If I had a store and I needed antiques for a display, I'd do business with Vintage, Inc., too! I started to wonder why anyone in her right mind would do business with silly little me. I ran my silly so-called business from a little house on a housing tract. I didn't know how to sell. I had no experience. I had barely any inventory. By the time I added up Vintage, Inc.'s assets and my shortcomings, I felt that I had nothing.

In my mind, I viewed Vintage, Inc., as the perfect business. I imagined men in white gloves placing antiques on conveyer belts that ran through that 50,000-square-foot warehouse. I pictured people packing orders and placing box after box onto gleaming trucks that whisked them away to stores all over the country.

I thought Vintage, Inc., had it made. I had no clue as to how to compete, and truthfully, I didn't really believe I could. Dejected, I kept making my calls, and I tried to figure out how to get my hands on $10 million in inventory. I was sure that the only way I could compete with Vintage, Inc., was to match it asset for asset, warehouse for warehouse—that is, until I met Patti.

Patti, the buyer for Macy's West in Los Angeles, actually took my call one day and immediately told me that she needed some vintage beds for a linen display and didn't have time to order from the East Coast. As I drove to meet Patti in L.A. the next day, I was hoping for a $3,000 to $5,000 order, which would have been a great month in those days. In our meeting, Patti requested vintage beds and accessories for two different department stores—an order that added up to $40,000! I was ecstatic; she even authorized an immediate deposit of $20,000.

We bribed some friends with pizza and beer, and together we delivered the Macy's order in two rented U-Haul trucks. I didn't own a truck with my logo emblazoned across the sides, and I didn't have uniformed delivery people in my employ. But when we made the deliveries, we laughed and joked with the Macy's staff. We were personable and fun, and we delivered the items on time and in perfect condition.

We had a great time delivering the order and even helped set up the displays. Patti seemed very pleased. I was thrilled. If only we could do this level of business on a regular basis. But did that mean we had to wait around until Patti had a tight timeline and couldn't order from Vintage, Inc.? Did I want to be a backup choice?

I had to be daring. I had to be bold. I invited Patti to lunch.

At lunch, I took a deep breath and asked Patti a question that had been burning me up inside for some time.

"Why did you choose to do business with me?"

"Because I like you. You're fun," Patti answered. She liked me. She thought I was fun. I had not imagined such a simple answer, but it emboldened me to ask another question.

"Why didn't you use Vintage, Inc.?"

The answer changed my life forever.

"David, I *hate* Vintage, Inc.," Patti replied. "The people there are so rude. They send broken items. They change orders without asking. They send things that are dirty and covered with dust. They're late with orders, and if I call to complain, they're rude to me. They just don't give a damn, and I hate dealing with them!"

In that instant, Vintage, Inc., fell right off that pedestal I had created in my mind. No longer was it the perfect company—far from it. But what really floored me was the realization that I did not *need* a 50,000-square-foot warehouse or $10 million in inventory. I had something more valuable, and that something was *fun*.

We did not have to compete with the big guys; we had to be ourselves. It really was that simple.

From that day forward, my whole sales approach changed. Instead of asking stores if they needed to purchase antiques or vintage display items, I made it clear that our business was a standout because of our attitude. I would start every sales call saying, "I know you need to buy these things anyway, so how about working with a company that's *fun* to do business with?"

Selling became fun. I could hear people's minds spinning when I let them know it would be fun to do business with us. What a concept! My confidence soared, and sales started rolling in. We were no longer just selling antiques. We were selling a fun experience. By daring to stand up and be counted, I had learned a key concept in business: People buy experiences. And those experiences don't have anything to do with money or warehouses. Anyone can build a successful business—and a World Famous brand—if he is just willing to stand out and stand up.

I tell you this story about our first big sale because it demonstrates what can happen when you dare to be authentically you. When you dare to stand up and be counted. When you dare to go after your marketplace, even if you're the new guy working out of your garage. When you dare to focus on what makes you different instead of trying to fit in. So raise your hand. You know the answer. You are worthy. You can succeed!

Dare to speak up.

Dare to stand out.

Dare to embrace and own that which makes you different.

Dare to go after the big clients—to go after your marketplace, despite the competition.

Dare to see your own unique value, beyond assets and income.

Dare to discover what makes your business unique.

Dare to knock on doors until one opens.

Dare to stand up and be counted.

CHAPTER 2

Dare to Stand Out

I am about to dare you to do something that is so contrary to human nature, something that is so revolutionary, that once you act on the dare, you'll never be the same. In fact, if you commit to this dare, not only will you be irrevocably changed, but you'll be World Famous. Are you ready for it?

I dare you to stand out.

What? You were expecting something more earth-shattering? What could be bigger, harder, or more challenging than going against your basic human instinct to fit in?

Throughout this journey, you will be faced with the decision to fit in or stand out. You'll have to fight the urge to follow the example set forth by other businesses in your industry, and you'll have to challenge yourself to embrace differentiation. As you build your very own World Famous brand identity, you'll have to get clarity about your business and express your business personality authentically. Your World Famous brand identity is dependent on your willingness to reveal what you believe in, what you stand for, and what's important to you. My dare encompasses all of this, because when you dare to stand out, you can accomplish all of the above and more.

Let's dig a little deeper so that you understand why daring you to stand out is perhaps the most life-altering dare anyone will ever challenge you to.

From birth on, we study our fellow humans to learn how to live on this planet. Our family, friends, teachers, and coworkers impart intricate systems of etiquette at every stage of our life. When we say the "wrong thing" or have the *audacity* to behave differently from the norm, our community rushes in to get us back in line. Through gentle reminders, punishment, or outright shunning, we quickly learn that in order to be accepted in our family, our neighborhood, our school, or our place of business, we *must fit in.* We do it accidentally. We follow rules, guidelines, and assumptions without realizing that we have a choice.

Following the status quo is also much easier than daring to be different or trying something new because we are able to walk a well-traveled path. Often we choose to do as others do simply because we just don't know how to do it another way, our own way. We can feel silly or frustrated when we try to carve out our own path, and so we just choose the easiest course and get on with it.

How many World Famous brand identities do *you* know that achieved success by fitting in? How many World Famous people do you know who became celebrities because they blended in with the rest of society?

I'll give you an example of how daring to stand out had a huge impact on my former business. One day we received a visual merchandising order from Macy's outside San Francisco. We had done business with Macy's before, but we had not serviced this particular store. We shipped the order promptly, so when the buyer called a few days later to say that it had not arrived, I was surprised. I knew that the order had been delivered, but I had no idea where it was.

One of the things we were known for was certainty; we *always* made sure that shipments arrived on time. Instead of asking the buyer to wait until we could sort out the problem, we shipped another order of the identical items, and requested a signature on delivery. A few days later, the buyer called again.

"We never received the order," he said, clearly frustrated. I knew that Macy's had received the second order because we had a signature from someone in the shipping department.

"I'm just 25 minutes away. I'll drive out there and figure this out," I offered.

When I pulled up to the Macy's receiving dock, I was amazed. It felt bigger than the store itself! I started searching through a sea of brown cardboard boxes, and that's when it hit me: Everyone shipped in brown cardboard boxes. I was supposed to be the expert at standing out from the crowd, and I was just like everyone else.

It took quite some time to find the orders, and when I returned to my office, I addressed the problem in our weekly brainstorm meeting.

"Listen, we have a problem. Everybody ships in brown cardboard boxes," I explained. "We're not standing out."

What we did next not only allowed our business to stand out but made us famous. We looked at every aspect of conventional shipping boxes and put our own spin on it. We started using white cardboard boxes with a photo of me on the outside and a bubble saying, "Here it is!" Even the handling instructions were different, stating, "Please treat this box like chocolate, but do not lick your hands."

We used red ink instead of black, and we posted a quiz on one side with silly questions like, "Who is the best-looking guy on this box?" We also added funny statements such as, "If you take this box to the correct department, you get to keep the bubble wrap and pop it yourself." We stood out from the pile, and our boxes were opened *first*. People got excited when they got our box. We never received another call from a client who couldn't find our order among all the others.

We also added our phone number to the box with the message, "If you like this box, call this number." Shipping personnel, husky-sounding union guys, would call up and leave us messages about how much they liked our boxes. Soon we became known as "the guys with the boxes," and people associated distinctive visual branding with our company.

I've been in the United States for 20 years now, and I have embraced the trailblazing way of life that is uniquely American. In fact, it was this courageous spirit that drew me here to begin with. Now imagine what might have happened to that American spirit if, instead of declaring their independence from England, the colonists had decided to pay their taxes and follow the rules of a faraway sovereignty. By nature they were adventurous; anyone who travels across vast, deep oceans in search of freedom, riches, or just a second chance has some guts.

Just as life is an adventure, business is also an adventure. And no matter what your circumstances, no matter how many times you have failed or lost or come up short, you can have your own adventure, too. In fact, you're already there. You picked up this book, you're reading it, and even though I dared you to defy convention and stand out, you didn't run scared. You're still here with me.

But what if you decide *not* to accept my dare? What will happen to your business, or your life, if you opt to forgo this journey—your adventure—and follow the status quo? What if, when it came time for the colonists to stand up—to stand out—for freedom, everyone had stayed home?

History is full of daring souls who acted when no one else would: artists who experimented with new forms and styles; leaders who fought for a better way of life; inventors who envisioned miraculous machines; doctors who worked to achieve the impossible; entrepreneurs who made something out of nothing. Your ancestry is full of remarkable accomplishments that may not have made the history books, but that were the stuff of legend within your own family. Would all of these grand tales have come to pass if the people behind them had decided not to make waves?

The truth is, no one ever became World Famous by blending in, nor did any business. Following the status quo leads only to more of the same, making us invisible. Yet even in America, where children are raised on the founding ideals of freedom, where a pioneering spirit pervades the culture, most people wouldn't think of standing out. Even with independence woven into the fabric of society, most Americans choose not to step outside the social norms of their community.

Remember the school dances? Remember how hard it was to be the first person on that giant, empty floor? Even if you did brave it and ask your date to dance, you certainly didn't show off those freestyle dance moves, no matter how many nights you had practiced them alone in your room.

Even in business, the need to fit in feels just as desperate as it did in junior high. As business owners and career innovators, we feel the need to add legitimacy to our goals and credibility to our brilliant ideas. We use the outward trappings of business to anchor our dream in reality, not really ever considering whether our business cards, voicemail messages, and web sites fit with who we are—and, more importantly, who we aspire to be. We have to be different, and being different means standing out.

Despite the fact that it took a massive amount of courage to start our business or launch our career in the first place, we fear that others will figure us out; our colleagues and competitors will be able to look into our eyes and see fear, inexperience, or poor judgment. So we search the Internet for articles on how to start a business and follow the bullet points one by one, we follow the guidelines and "rules" that we learned in business school, and we look to other businesses as examples and do exactly as they do. Is it any wonder that most businesses are hard to tell apart?

Very often entrepreneurs carry an employee mentality over into their new business. It's as if the ghost of bosses past hovers over them, feeding their insecurity and a desire to keep everything on the straight and narrow rather than shake things up. The same can be said for managers, CEOs, and sales directors—virtually anyone who chooses to be a follower rather than a leader.

Here's the conundrum: It's human nature to want to fit in, yet it's also human nature to *choose things that stand out.* People make purchasing decisions based on what resonates with them, what makes an impression on them, and you can't make an impression when you look and behave exactly like everyone else.

Let me be perfectly clear: This is not about standing out for the sake of standing out; it is about daring yourself to be uniquely you. As you develop your World Famous brand identity, you will approach each aspect of brand building with this dare firmly in mind. As you explore what makes your business unique and the personality and attitude of your brand, your willingness to stand out from the crowd is imperative. Daring to stand out will allow you to truly reveal the essence of your business and to find the most genuine, meaningful, powerful answers to what makes your brand World Famous. You need to carry this daring feeling all the way through all the steps, so that when you get to the final step of engaging your marketplace, you can use it to push your efforts to the next level.

Dare to shake things up.

Dare to ruffle feathers, try something new, and take a chance.

Dare to be authentic. Genuine. Real.

Dare to apply meaning to your brand.

Dare to do more than just "a perfectly fine job."

Dare to rise to the occasion. Seek a higher purpose. Become World Famous.

Dare to join this adventure.

Dare to stand out.

CHAPTER 3

Dare to Be
Authentically Different

At the heart of this dare is a call for authenticity—*your* authenticity. Because when you strive to look like or keep up with the guy next door, it is often at the expense of your true self. In branding, trust is vital. But how can you expect customers to trust your message, your product, and your company when they are built on a desire to blend in with others? It's like putting on a costume; no one can see the real you, but people know you're in there. It makes them nervous and sends a message that you are not comfortable in your own skin.

When you strive to fit in or fit in by default, your brand cannot resonate with consumers. Your brand identity needs to mean something to your marketplace. Again, most businesses do a fine job, run a tight ship, and work like dogs, but they simply aren't meaningful to consumers. Their brand doesn't resonate with their marketplace in a way that compels consumers to do business with them, that special something that often can't be named, that thing that inspires consumers to relate to a brand, to *love* a brand.

So you have a massive opportunity.

In business, you need to do more than is expected of you. You need to go beyond your job description, your investors' requirements, even your own initial goals. You need to connect with your marketplace so that people are engaged in the experience of doing business with you. People need more from you than your products or services; they need you to wake them up, charm them, make them think, cajole them, tease them, and make them sit up and notice your business.

What are the businesses and brands that do this for *you*? Which businesses do you love? Which businesses excite you? Which businesses ask something different of you from other run-of-the-mill businesses? In your opinion, do any of these businesses value fitting in? Do any of the brands you love appear to be mimicking other businesses? Do they fall into the status quo and expect you to "find them" and "figure them out"?

We tend to emulate others without really thinking about it. Can you think of one or two ways in which your business is pretending to be something it is not? Or, are there aspects of your business that you just haven't given much thought to, preferring instead to follow suit so that you can get on with your master plan?

Do you use the same PowerPoint templates for your presentations over and over? Does your office fall under the corporate veil of sameness, with nondescript décor and a waiting room that is hard to tell apart from the other waiting rooms in your building? Did you record a voicemail based on what you hear when you call other companies?

If your business were compared to an airline, would it be more like United or American, or would it resonate with a marketplace the way Virgin Atlantic or Southwest does? If your business were compared to an ice cream company, would it be more like the generic brand or like Ben & Jerry's? Businesses can be standardized to the point where this becomes an Achilles heel.

Are you selling yourself short? Are you approaching aspects of your business without acknowledging the choices you have, as if you were worried about rocking the boat or being laughed at for being different? Are you holding yourself back? Do you pass out boring business cards? Does your letterhead seem utilitarian? What about your brochures? Do they look like those created by every other company that does what you do, or do they uniquely represent your brand identity? What is fueling your decision making? Is it insecurities like the fear of appearing unprofessional or underqualified, or are you boldly making a statement that inspires your marketplace?

What is your sales approach? Does it border on boring? Is it steady, old-school, and serious? What are the rules of your company? Do they inspire you and your staff members to be vibrant and authentic whenever they touch the world that is your marketplace? How about your voicemail message and your web site? What do they have in common with the voicemail messages and web sites of other businesses in your industry? What do they have in common with those of other businesses in general?

How many of the systems, processes, practices, and behaviors of your business emulate others rather than being a *wow* that presents the energy and attitude of your own unique, World Famous brand?

Maybe those commonalities *are* part of your unique personality, your authentic self. But have you ever thought about it? Isn't it possible that you buy, say, and do things just because everyone else does? You are a unique and authentic person, and your business is unique and authentic. Let it shine.

Another reason businesses often choose sameness over standing out is the belief that it will legitimize their business. Behaving just like the other businesses in your industry proves that you are part of the club; you belong there just as much as the other guy. So the focus is on adhering to the norm and improving on it, rather than on shattering it to bits. This is true on every level, but especially with seemingly small aspects of business, where it may seem odd or amateurish to do things differently from others.

I'll give you an example. Early on in my business, I was able to afford a computer and a printer, but not the *envelope attachment* for my printer. All of my envelopes had to be handwritten. Oh, how I coveted that envelope attachment. I couldn't wait to get it. I was embarrassed every time I sent out handwritten correspondence. I wanted my business to look professional like everyone else's, right down to the printed envelopes.

The day I could finally afford the envelope attachment for my printer, I felt as though I had officially joined "the club." Since I had the appropriate equipment, I knew that my business was finally legitimate. I was thrilled when I sent out the first batch of mailings. At last I fit in. Boy, did I ever. The response to my mailings went down 75 percent! I was fitting in so well that no one noticed me among *all the other printed envelopes*. Fitting in cost me dearly, and I'm certain it is costing you as well.

Even small dares can generate huge dividends, if they come from a place of authenticity. So rather than focus all (or any) of your energy on legitimizing your business, find a way to set your business apart from your competitors. Don't waste your time on the status quo. It's boring, and it's costly.

Have you ever been to a swap meet or flea market? You know, the kind that has one T-shirt vendor for every ten booths? Talk about a saturated market. Each vendor has a table covered with piles of shirts, all displayed in the same fashion, and with many of the same designs. Invariably, there is a sign that says something like, "Ten T-shirts for $20!" Sounds like a good deal, right? So why don't you buy one—or ten? Because they are all the same. They blur into each other, so that not one of them is memorable.

So why do all the T-shirt vendors offer the same deal? Because they feel they *have to*. The other vendors are doing it, so everyone follows suit, believing that the only way to motivate the market is to offer a rock-bottom price. Wrong. Because the T-shirt vendors all look and act the same, T-shirts have become a commodity. And the problem is that the market, not the vendor, dictates a commodity's price.

Are the T-shirt vendors doing great business? Just by looking at their booths, you can tell that money is tight: the same tired slogans and designs, slashed prices, and a bored look on the salesperson's face. Makes you want to run right over and buy the lot of them, right? Not so much. But would you notice a T-shirt vendor with a great brand identity, perhaps with T-shirts displayed on dress forms, and a price that's higher than the other vendors charge, but still quite fair? Probably. If she had great *different* T-shirts, you might actually buy one. You might even pay $10 or $20 or even $30 for just one T-shirt, or $50 for three.

Unless you are a T-shirt vendor, you probably don't consider your business to be in the same league as these swap meet regulars. But we all fall victim to this mimicking behavior, sometimes accidentally. How many times have you made a phone call and suffered through a cookie-cutter voicemail message? Perhaps you ignored it completely until you heard the beep. Either way the message doesn't work; it annoys or bores you, and so you don't listen.

Each time you opt to fit in rather than stand out, you are missing an opportunity to connect with your market. It's as if you are adding another piece of camouflage to your business. The more camouflage you add, the more difficult it is for your market to find you. Pretty soon, you're just another booth in a vast sea of T-shirt vendors.

Understand, I'm not advocating attracting attention for attention's sake. Standing out from the crowd must come from a place of honesty in order for it to be effective. So when I dare you to have the courage to stand out, I am not referring to crass, show-off behavior. No flashing the paparazzi and no ridiculous feuds; think less about celebrity tactics and more about setting your business apart from other businesses. And the best way to do that is to be 100 percent real.

Ask yourself, how many times have I followed protocol when it didn't fit my personality? How many ways have I compromised my own values or ideas because it was just easier to do so? How many times have I sought answers outside of myself, rather than finding the answer within?

The truth is, we equate fitting in with likability. We care about what people think of us. We care a lot. In fact, this instinct is so strong in humans that we often set our own truth aside in order to fit in; that little voice inside can be so easily ignored. Whenever you dare to stand out from the crowd, you will *always* attract a certain amount of negative response. Some people will laugh at you. Some people will ridicule you. Some people will tell you that you are foolish, silly, or wrong. But those people are not your market; they are simply there to test your authenticity—and your resolve.

In most cases, your fears are bigger than the reality. When you confidently own it, you are less likely to meet adversity and are less likely to hear the answer no. You must dare in spite of your fears, because they are not based in truth.

Remember, unless you own a company like mine, where my own personality is synonymous with my business personality, your individual personality is not at issue here. The persona of your business is the task at hand. So if you're starting to worry because you're really quite shy, or because you are part of a large, diverse company with many personalities, remember that this is about your brand identity, not you. Your brand can be like an alter ego, as long as it is authentic to your business and the personality of your business.

Always remember that not everyone has to like your brand, but your customers have to *love* it. That thing about your business that some people don't like may be the very thing that your specific target market—your superniche—absolutely loves. Why trade a customer's love and devotion for mere likability?

Besides, a certain amount of "negative commentary" is good for you, as it keeps a conversation going about your brand. Yet most people would do just about anything to avoid criticism. Too often, we are silent when we should be shouting in agreement or opposition, we are still when we should take action, and we are willing to make sacrifices of ourselves in order to belong. But tell me, is this why you went into business? To fit in? To be liked? To live the same life as the guy next door? My guess is that your answer is a resounding no. So what are you going to do about it?

The myriad ways in which your business touches the world that is your marketplace must be congruous with your brand identity, and by the time you reach the last of the five steps, you'll have a clearly defined, vibrant brand that's ready to make its debut. In the final step, I'll help you use your brand profile to engage your market uniquely and brilliantly, so that all those aspects of your business that for the time being mirror other businesses are transformed into engaging experiences for your marketplace.

But first, you need to get even *more* daring. You have to dare to be different.

Dare to challenge all of your preconceived notions.

Dare to look at each way your business touches the world with new eyes—to engage your market differently, and brilliantly.

Dare to be powerful, not predictable; to rise above being a commodity.

Dare to chart your own course rather than follow the path set forth by your competitors.

Dare to seek legitimacy in the heart and soul of your business, rather than in the trappings of operating a business.

Dare to be bold, to be brave.

Dare to be yourself, your authentic self, in business and in life.

Dare to stand out from the crowd, to break free of the status quo.

Dare!

A dare is not a request; it's a challenge. A dare is not a simple task; it's a courageous act. Daring allows us to break free of those silent demons that hold us back. To dare is to shine. To dare is to win. To dare is to stand out as the only choice.

Daring is not an item to check off on your to-do list. Daring is an attitude, a way of life. You didn't buy this book because you want your business to just do well. You bought this book because you want your business to be World Famous.

To be World Famous within your market, you must be daring. You must challenge yourself to notice when you are inadvertently conforming. You must search for your authentic business identity. You must dare to stand out; it is the only way you will be considered the obvious choice. The *only* choice. Standing out as the only choice in the hearts and minds of your market is the key to being World Famous in business.

The first step in creating a World Famous brand identity is to cultivate a culture of daring in your company, beginning with yourself. You must dare to stand out. Dare to circumvent human nature, our natural desire to fit in, join the club, and adopt behaviors just like everyone else. This step is paramount.

The dichotomy is that human nature leans toward fitting in

with societal norms, yet humans prefer to choose people, businesses, and things that stand out. You must understand this conundrum and dare yourself to be different—authentically different, based on your own unique style, values, personality, and goals.

When you dare to be real in every aspect of your business, you discover new opportunities to engage your marketplace. From your voicemail message to your marketing materials to your web site, all the ways in which your business comes in contact with your marketplace must be authentic, congruous with your brand, and engaging. When you dare to be real and abandon the status quo, you ensure that all of your systems are in keeping with your brand identity.

When you dare to stand out and be real, you become the only choice. You become World Famous.

Success is a decision, not a stroke of luck. If you are to succeed in business, you need to dare to stand out, dare to break free of the safety of emulating others. Dare to be authentic; dare to be different. Everything is riding on it.

So I dare you. I dare you to search for greatness in all that you do. Now dare yourself.

Exercises

The desire to fit in is a deep and complicated aspect of human nature, and even if you think you've got it all figured out, you'll benefit from these exercises. Plus, they're fun!

1. If your company did not have a dress code, what would you wear to work every day? To meetings? To business dinners? To events?

2. Describe three events in your personal and/or business life in which you summoned up the courage to go against the grain. Include why you chose to be daring and how you benefited from the experience.

3. If you woke up tomorrow incapable of feeling embarrassment, humiliation, or even fear, what aspect of your business would you change immediately? Now make a list of the other

changes you would institute, or tasks you would perform, if you had no concern for the outcome.

4. Imagine your place of business as if you are entering it for the first time. How can you tell what type of business it is? Which aspects of your business—décor, stationery, signage, and so on—reveal the essence of your brand identity?

5. If you blindfolded one of your customers and then escorted him to a similar business, could he tell that he was no longer at your establishment? If so, what would be the giveaway?

6. Surprise! Your staff is now capable of accomplishing any task you assign them. What is the first thing on your to-do list, perhaps something that you've been putting off for quite some time?

7. What would you like people to think of when they think about your World Famous brand? What would you like your business to be known for?

8. What bores you about the businesses you frequent? What are your pet peeves about some of the businesses you *have to* endure?

9. What kind of money do you want to make? Beyond money, what kind of adventures do you want to have with your business?

10. What do you want written on your tombstone?

11. What great big, juicy, outrageous goals might you have? What are the *secret* goals that you have been afraid to say out loud—until now?

12. What does it mean to you when I say, "World Famous brand"? If your brand were World Famous, in what way would your company be different? Be specific. Would your products or services change? Would your staff or workspace change? What about your attitude?

Keep your answers close as you begin to work on your brand profile, as you'll want to refer back to them in further exercises. (Download your *free* brand profile document at www.worldfamous company.com, press the BRAND PROFILE tab, and enter code WF001.) You may be surprised at how your answers to these questions change and expand, getting bolder and brighter as you go through this book. Remember, this is a journey, and you can always go back and revise your answers later on. This is *your* life and *your* business. This is *your* World Famous brand.

And we're off!

STEP
2

Discover the Power of the Superniche

"Less is more."

—ROBERT BROWNING

Why do we think we have to market to 8 million, or 50 million, or 10 billion people in order to succeed? Because we are satisfying a misunderstood conventional wisdom that it is better to have as big a market as possible. But it goes deeper than that. The truth is that we're afraid to narrow our focus because choosing a smaller, more defined market may limit our earning potential.

The desire to market to the entire world results in marketing to no one. Whether you're attempting to market to everyone on the planet or you're expanding your product line outside of your comfort zone in order to sell even more *stuff* to everyone on the planet, it's a "superstore" mentality. What you need is a superniche mentality, the ability to focus on your unique market with laser-beam precision. Once you've established your brand as the only choice, people outside of your superniche will gravitate toward your brand, thereby expanding your reach in an authentic, organic way that yields long-term success.

On paper, marketing to a vast market seems like common sense. More customers equals more products or services sold, equals more income and more success. What's wrong with that? Nothing, except that this scenario depends on our getting the customers in the first place, which is pretty tough to do if we have no idea how to connect with them and inspire them to do business with us. Think about the phrase "pushing buttons." Well, pushing buttons requires resources. And no one, not even Bill Gates, has the resources to market to everyone.

Trying to appeal to a broad market leads only to a depletion of resources—creative, financial, and human—and a loss of customers who no longer feel that you are marketing directly to them. So while you're busy killing yourself trying to market to the whole world, your ideal customers are choosing a different brand that speaks directly to them. The end result is that you are exhausted and broke, wondering where you went wrong.

Dare to define and commit to one specific marketplace, a *superniche* that you know inside and out. Beyond demographics and deeper than basic customer characteristics, a superniche is a well-honed, carefully defined group that not only *wants* your brand but *needs* it. And the people in this group need it because it helps to define—prove, even—who they are and what they stand for.

Based on demographics and psychographics, the heart of your superniche market is the people that you enjoy doing business with. You can actually choose to work with people and businesses that you are comfortable with, those you prefer, the people whom you understand, who respect you and appreciate you, and whom you can call your own.

Declaring and committing to a superniche is wildly important because without a superniche, most businesses fail to prosper. You must know who "your people" are and what they're all about. The better you know them, the better able you are to determine what they will like, what they will appreciate, and what will inspire them to feel connected to your business.

Whenever a client tells me that her market is everyone, I ask, "Oh, so that means prisoners too, right? Which kind do you prefer? Murderers or bank robbers?" She knows I'm being facetious, so it doesn't take long for her to realize that it's time to make a decision. Marketing to everyone is dangerous. Marketing to a superniche is exciting and profitable.

Think of it as throwing a party for your best friends. You know what kind of food, music, and entertainment they like, and you have a good idea of what will constitute a great time in their hearts and minds. If your nearest and dearest are having the time of their lives, then their friends and neighbors will want in on the party. Happy people are contagious. Fun is contagious. Energy is contagious. When your superniche is energized by your brand, when the people in it gain pleasure from choosing your brand, others outside of your superniche will get in line to share in the fun.

When you dare to choose a specific market, you let go of your need to be liked by everyone. Sometimes, in the search for likability, it's easy to forget that some of the most successful brands are actually disliked by certain groups. Take Fox News, for example. Hugely successful, the Fox News brand is as much about the superniche that tunes in every night as it is about those who wouldn't dream of watching a single second of its programs. In fact, those who buy into the brand that is Fox News *take pleasure* in the fact that many people dislike the brand. It makes them feel like part of a special club. If everyone loved Fox News, would the network's raving fans rave as loudly? Probably not.

It's human nature to try to appeal to as many people as possible. Of course you want to sell the latest "must have" product or service, a phenomenon of major proportions. I know you wouldn't be reading this book if you didn't have ambitious goals for your business. But the best way to reach those goals is by defining your market as tightly as possible, then focusing on it like a laser beam. Do you want to be the person who is afraid to miss out on an opportunity, or the person who *creates* opportunity everywhere you go?

Even the real superstores didn't start out marketing to every Tom, Dick, and Harry. Take Target and Wal-Mart, for example. Both are successful superstores marketing a wide range of products to a seemingly broad group of people. But how many people do you know who frequent both stores equally? Some people are "Target people," and some people are "Wal-Mart people." What makes two superstores so different that people would identify with one rather than the other?

Target was created to appeal to a very specific demographic: those who already frequented the upscale department stores owned by the Dayton family. Target's superniche was, and remains, middle-class or affluent consumers looking for high-quality, trendy products at discounted prices. Wal-Mart, on the other hand, was founded by Sam Walton and began as a five-and-dime discount store. From the beginning and to this day, the Walton brand was all about low prices. Wal-Mart's superniche is the lower-income family looking for the lowest prices, regardless of quality.

For the people in Target's superniche, the brand's stylish and hip persona appeals to their own image of themselves, whereas those in Wal-Mart's superniche do not relate to those attributes. Likewise, Wal-Mart's focus on delivering a cheap product is a turnoff to Target's superniche. Target's superniche wants economy, style, and choice. Wal-Mart's superniche wants cheap, no frills, and a sense of community.

While both Wal-Mart and Target now have actual superstores, they didn't start out that way. Both Target and Wal-Mart began with one store and focused primarily on their superniche. Though both corporations have attempted to expand their reach, even the big guys know that they have to stay true to their brand and consider the desires of their superniche first and foremost.

Another example of a "superstore" with a superniche is Amazon.com. At first it was all about the books. Now you can get pretty much anything you want on Amazon, making it one of the first online superstores. But adding products and partnerships was a gradual process for Amazon. Once, it was the go-to place for online book shopping. Now, it is the go-to place for almost *any* online shopping.

Amazon's business model really sold the brand, and that model has been maintained and improved upon through the online retailer's expansion. Throughout the growth process, Amazon stayed focused on its superniche, the customer who wanted access to a wide range of books, but also wanted the opinion of readers and the type of helpful recommendations that one might receive when browsing a brick-and-mortar bookstore. Amazon's super- niche wants to pay less and feel smart about it. Its members are not cheap, but discerning. Informed shoppers, Amazon fans just don't see the need to pay more for an identical product. In short, Ama- zon's superniche is discerning, smart, and informed.

Amazon.com is also a perfect example of a "superstar." Right off the bat, Amazon's founder, Jeff Bezos, got a lot of press for his business plan, his business model, and, most importantly, his story. People love a great garage-to-millionaire tale, and Bezos was imme- diately pegged as an innovator. Inspired by his story, people logged on and bought books, thereby aligning their story with his. The story and the innovation made Amazon.com a superstar, and its raving fans enabled it to become a superstore.

Remember the quote from the introduction? The one you have posted where you can read it every day? *There are masses of people just waiting to do business with you once they are so inspired.* The important thing to understand is the difference between "masses" and "everyone."

You can absolutely still have a huge market, and you can still be the biggest brand in your industry. But a large market is different from a broad market, in that a large market is about size and a broad market is about size *and range.* As long as your superniche is tight and focused, it can be as huge as you want it to be.

So let go of the misconception that everyone is a potential customer whom you need to win over, or that the most lucrative market should be your primary focus. Instead, focus on the group of people or businesses that you most identify with and understand. Set the charts and statistics aside for now and go with your gut, that which you *just know.*

Take a deep breath and relax, knowing that there are many markets that are open to your business, and that you get to have your pick. And take comfort in the fact that when you choose to do business with a market you feel good about doing business with, inspiring that market can be effortless. In the next few chapters, you will discover exactly how to do just that.

CHAPTER 4

The Secret to Why People Buy

Why do I choose Virgin Atlantic over another airline? Why do you choose, say, an upscale restaurant over a fast-food joint? Why do people buy what they buy? Why do you buy what you buy?

The reason for all purchasing decisions is: We buy things that fit the "story" of our lives. Not our life stories. *The story of our lives.* Specifically, this is how we see ourselves and who we aspire to be, our values, and what we believe our worth to be. It's as if you are giving your customers a voice, empowering them to claim the vision they have for their own life. Branding is not about selling; it's about championing the people in your market and offering them a space where they can be their true, authentic selves.

What voice are you giving your people? How are you empowering them? What message are you sending that enables them to feel free, to express who they are, and to claim their dreams as reality? Your mission in business is to create a haven for your customers, real or imagined, that allows them to be exactly who they are. To build a World Famous brand identity is to commit to this higher calling, to truly inspire your market at its very core. The result is a customer base that is compelled to do business with you, as if saying, "Where have you been all my life?"

World Famous brands love their people and want to make them feel good. I love my people, my branding clients, and my seminar participants, and I know the story of their lives. They're daring, think-outside-the-box people who are looking for a voice amidst the cubicles, wanting to come out from behind the desk and shout their ideas from the rooftops. Like you, the people and businesses I consult with want to stand out; they want to grab the attention of the marketplace authentically. Knowing them gives them a voice; it makes them feel comfortable enough to speak up for what they want—and *that* makes them want to do business with me.

In defining your superniche, you give your own people a voice. What is the result? People are inspired to do business with you because they know that you understand the story of their lives. The same is true for any authentic brand that is grounded in this knowledge.

Starbucks gives a voice to people who want to feel welcome and comfortable in a café, even if they want to sit there all day. Virgin Atlantic gives a voice to people who want to feel like hip, maverick stars when they travel, rather than like cattle. Polo Ralph Lauren gives a voice to people who want to feel that they were born with a silver spoon in their mouth, even if they were not. When we worked with Polo Ralph Lauren, we focused on giving a story to the whole concept of prestige, providing props that evoked that lifestyle, such as gentlemen's accessories, trophies, and vintage luggage. Nautica gives a voice to those who are in search of sophistication and a life of leisure and adventure. When we worked with Nautica, we focused on that feeling of being out on the open water, incorporating sailboats and other nautical-style props.

Which brands give you a voice? Which brands help you become *more you*? Examining your own brand loyalties will help you understand why people buy. Look at how each business you patronize fits into the story of your life, and you will see that the brands you love also love you. The brands you love give you a voice.

This is the true power of a superniche, the power to inspire your market in a meaningful way. I know it may seem like a huge undertaking, but I am hoping you will realize that this approach to brand building is actually the simplest, most effective way of achieving success, because just by *considering* your business and how it can give voice to your market, you are elevating the stature of your brand. Just by asking these questions of yourself and your business, you are connecting with your market on a deeply personal level. And it won't cost you a dime.

CHAPTER 5

Demographics in 10 Minutes or Less

The best way to understand your superniche is to visualize a funnel, wide at the top and narrow at the bottom. The widest end represents your broadest reach, the demographic of your superniche. The narrow end represents a more specific group, the psychographic of your superniche. Your psychographic further tightens your focus within your demographic. For example, dentists with over 1,000 patients (demographic) who are cutting-edge, sophisticated, and contemporary (psychographic).

Discovering your superniche begins with choosing the demographic of your marketplace. If it's been a few years since you dusted off your business plan, demographics classify people (and businesses) in ways that can be measured.

Your demographic might be thirtysomething professionals with an average annual income of $100,000 and twice that in student loans, for example. Or it might be teenagers living in affluent suburbs with a single parent, or married empty nesters paying for their kids' college and their own retirement. Same-sex parents of two or more adopted children. California optometrists with at least

200 patients, homeowners with an income above $85,000, or even astronomers who are members of Overeaters Anonymous. These are groups that can be described in measurable terms.

What measurable characteristics best describe your demographic? For some businesses, religion is the primary concern. For others, the top factors are gender, geographic area, or education. A dentist, for example, might define his demographic by first language and/or socioeconomic status. Choose the demographic that is important to you, that makes the most sense for your business *and* the goals that you have for your business.

It's tempting to labor over demographics, but I don't advise it. You know your business, so I'm going to assume that you know the general demographic of your marketplace. It's not like you're going to get this wrong, unless you haven't been paying attention to your clientele or haven't a clue about the benefits of your product or service. I'm a big fan of timed exercises because they force you to trust your gut instincts and leave little or no time for second-guessing yourself. Choosing a demographic is the perfect exercise to try to complete in less than 10 minutes because—come on, say it with me—*you can't sell to everyone!*

A common mistake that businesses make is focusing on the most lucrative demographic, even when it's not a good fit. While profit is obviously a major goal of business, you won't achieve your financial goals if you go against your instincts and choose money over passion. Of course, sometimes the demographic that resonates with you is also highly lucrative. But either way, going with your gut—and your heart—is the surest path to greatness.

I always encourage my clients to consider the customers they like best and understand, those they relate to, connect with, or simply do best with, rather than the bottom line when choosing a demographic focus. It might not be the most lucrative on paper, but it has unlimited potential because it can stimulate your passion. There was a time when I thought I *had* to be in business with certain people, people who were not good for my mental or spiritual health. If doing business with some people or companies gives you a bad feeling, if every time you do business with them, you feel as though you died a little, then this is not your market. And it most certainly is not your superniche.

Business is so much more enjoyable—and profitable—when you can talk effortlessly about your market. You know the people in it, you like them, and you respect them. More importantly, you want to do great things for them. You want to touch their hearts and minds. You want to inspire them.

If you go with a profitable demographic on that basis alone, you may find out that you cannot stand the people that make up that market. They get on your nerves. They're rude, or you just don't understand them. They take every ounce of your energy and give nothing back. Are you going to do a good job for them? Will you seek them out in hopes of reaching them on an emotional level, or will you avoid them like the plague?

While it does not have to be your primary concern, the type of people and companies you like to do business with is worth serious consideration. It's part of what builds that true pipeline connecting your business with your superniche and your superniche with your bank account.

So, the good news is, you have to focus on only one demographic. The bad news is, you have to choose one demographic. It never fails; the moment of decision always gives my clients anxiety. They say, "What if I choose the wrong demographic?" and "Wouldn't it be safer if I focused on lots of demographics?" No. (I usually cut them off right away before they get too caught up in this line of thinking.)

It makes sense that you would want to hedge your bets. It's human to fight this process, because once you commit to a demographic, your resource will be focused on that group and that group alone. I have worked with thousands of people who have been through this same process, and many of them were reluctant to choose just one demographic. It's sort of like skydiving: a highly charged, adrenalin-filled experience that, once you touch the ground, proves to be hugely satisfying and life-changing.

It's tempting to choose more than one demographic to focus on. No one wants to be wrong. But again, it's all about resources. Every person and every business has a limit to how much time, energy, creativity, money, and focus it can give to something. Building your pipeline requires your full attention. Each pipeline requires an investment of time, money, and resources. So build one pipeline at a time. Later, when your superniche is rewarding you by pumping lots of cash through your pipeline into your bank account, you can begin to think about identifying a new superniche.

When your demographic is well defined, it's easy to give it your full attention. If you have more than one demographic on deck, your efforts are split in two, or three, or four—wait, are you really thinking *four*? Stop right now and make a choice. Get out the timer and do the following 10-minute demographics exercise, keeping the focus on your gut, not your pocketbook.

Ten-Minute Exercise

What follows is a series of questions to help you build the demographic profile of your superniche in 10 minutes or less. You've got 10 minutes and 10 questions spread among the 6 categories. Go with it. Write down the first answer that comes to mind, and then move on to the next question. You can always refine your answers later. Ready, set, go!

1. If you are already in business, describe your favorite customers in basic terms. What do they have in common? If you are in the start-up phase, move on to the next question.

2. Describe the type of person who would need or want your product or service. For example, you might choose entrepreneurs, athletes, chefs, teachers, parents, the disabled, senior citizens, librarians, college students, or some other such group.

3. List the basic facts about your ideal customer, such as age, gender, marital status, socioeconomic status, and education level.

4. What is the geographic location of your average customer? If it is significant to your business, what type of dwelling does your average customer live in? For example, does she rent an apartment or a house, or does she own a condo, house, or farm?

5. How do most of your customers conduct business with you? For example, do they purchase products or services over the Internet, in person, or through the mail?

6. In an ideal world, what type of people or businesses do you wish you could do business with? Does this demographic fit the profile of your average customer? What's missing?

Next, take all the answers and put them into one list. Do any of the answers seem out of place? Are there any measurable characteristics that seem to be missing from the list? Remember to avoid adding new people or businesses to your demographic profile. And when in doubt, choose those you love to work with. Hang on to your list. You'll come back to it when you put it all together on your brand profile.

CHAPTER 6

Psychographics: Breathing Life Into Your Brand

Psychographics well utilized can turn a market into raving fans. Psychographics put a face, a heart, and a mind to the demographic you have chosen to do business with, breathing life and opportunity into your business and your brand.

The *American Heritage Dictionary* defines psychographics as "the use of demographics to study and measure attitudes, values, lifestyles, and opinions, as for marketing purposes." Psychographics define your market using aspirations and feelings rather than statistics. Demographics define your market "on paper," and psychographics define your market in real life. The psychographic of your superniche is one of the most important aspects of your business, and it will have an impact on the personality and attitude of your brand.

When you think of a person's life story versus the story of his life, it's similar to the concept of demographics versus psycho-

graphics. While it's quite possible that a person's demographic profile could be the reason behind a purchasing decision, in truth it's
a combination of demographics and psychographics.

For example, the fact that a person has two children of driving
age is the demographic aspect of that person that may create the
need to purchase a new vehicle. However, the person's values, frustrations, and aspirations—the psychographic aspect—are the determining factors in *what type of vehicle* this parent of teenagers might
choose. If the parent values style (i.e., pleasing his trend-conscious
teenagers) over resale value, he might purchase a hip, more expen-
sive car. Or, if he is frustrated about gas prices and worried about
global warming, he might choose a fuel-efficient hybrid. Or, if this
parent is feeling the pinch of a midlife crisis, he may give his kids
the minivan and snap up a convertible for himself!

So you see, the fact that the person in this example had two
teenagers at home makes him a likely candidate for a new car. His
life story is the clue to his needs. But how he views the world, his
aspirations, what he values, and what frustrates him will determine
whether he fits into the superniche of the Mercedes, the Prius, or
the Corvette. The story of his life provides the clues to his desires.

When considering psychographics, always keep in mind that
the story of our lives is forever unfolding. As a person learns and
grows, the stories may change. For example, it's possible that a
person who once needed a big "look at me" sports car could grow
up and become a person who is comfortable driving a hybrid or a
minivan. And part of her early story may influence her current
buying decisions, so that her hybrid (or minivan) *has* to have all
of the bells and whistles, just like her beloved sports car. It's still
the psychographics that stimulate the target market, the superniche.

Remember, many businesses are not focusing on the psychographic of the marketplace they wish to inspire, and that's why so
many of them are bland and forgettable. It's also the reason why so
many businesses and professionals have to work extra hard to make
the sales they need. Now that you know the power of identifying
the psychographic of your superniche, do you see how you have a
tremendous advantage over other businesses in your industry?

The great American fashion designer Ralph Lauren invented the lifestyle brand and is considered the godfather of lifestyle branding, which is a brand that embodies the psychographic of its customers. The Polo Ralph Lauren brand is not about one product, but about a refined, sophisticated, luxury lifestyle. It appeals to a very specific echelon of people. The brand suggests a lifestyle of considerable means and impressive heritage.

If there is such a thing as American royalty, it is encapsulated in the Polo Ralph Lauren brand. Capturing the essential features of a rare breed of refinement, excellence, and prestige, the brand suggests a renowned family name, a top-notch education, and all the trappings of culture and class. Polo Ralph Lauren is for those who live this life and for those who *aspire* to live this life.

Each product, from the iconic polo shirt to home décor, is designed to transport the customer into the prestigious world of Ralph Lauren. This wildly successful, flawless brand certainly knows how to stir up, inspire, and stimulate a very specific desire, one of heritage, good breeding, lineage, and class.

Polo Ralph Lauren knows its superniche so intimately that the company can push its customer's buttons with both hands tied behind its back! In fact, even on its web site, it states its aims: "Ralph Lauren has always stood for providing quality products, creating worlds and inviting people to take part in our dream." *Inviting people to take part in our dream.* This is exactly why Ralph Lauren is the godfather of lifestyle branding.

If your brand is to become World Famous, you must identify the unique group of people and businesses that want the dream that your business can provide, and then invite them in. Your brand identity is simply an invitation into a world that you create in the image of your customer. The genius of Ralph Lauren is that his brand represents something that people aspire to be like, rather than something that they already are. Even his wealthy, old-money fans buy into the brand because it embodies the best aspects of their luxury lifestyle.

Remember, this is Ralph Lauren's world, or, as his web site states, "our dream." He grew up as Ralph Lifshitz in the Bronx, far from the life he lives now. Polo Ralph Lauren is as much about the fantasy lifestyle he held while he was growing up as it is about the customers who aspire to live that lifestyle. He invented his own story, and he understood that other people would want to buy into that story, too. Ralph Lauren understood that people, regardless of their economic status, would purchase his brand because it spoke to their highest version of themselves. What could be more inspiring than that?

Your World Famous brand hinges on your ability to tap into the psychographics of your specific market. What do your customers aspire to be? What do they value most? What turns them on, lights them up, and fills them with joy? What frustrates them most, scares them just a little, or worries them a lot? Who are the people that will accept when you invite them into *your* dream?

Exercise: Fun with Psychographics!

The next step in building your superniche is applying a psychographic filter to your demographic. You're tightening your focus, refining the market until it represents the unique characteristics of the people who would most want to do business with you. Have fun with this process. Imagine that you are a screenwriter developing characters for a movie, or a director casting that movie, or a judge on *American Idol* in search of the ideal customer.

What follows are a series of short exercises to help you get your creative juices flowing. It's helpful to do this exercise with a team, so gather your advisers, your staff, or your business coach and start brainstorming. Here's a hint: Do the exercises in order for best results. Have at it!

1. I'm going to give you a huge head start by feeding you loads of descriptions. Take a look at the list, and circle the words or phrases that *best describe* your ideal customer. This could be the customer you already have, or the customer you aspire to have.

Use this list as a jumping-off point to brainstorm other words that describe the personality and attitudes of the customers in your demographic that you would most like to attract. If you're stuck, think about how you would like your customers to feel and start there.

Remember, you're looking for the psychographic of *your* superniche, which means that you also need to consider your business or your offering. For example, a daring entrepreneur may be shy when it comes to dancing, and a friendly pet owner might also relate to being a frustrated and outraged air traveler. When choosing words, please don't limit yourself to the lists of words in this book. They are simply designed to help you brainstorm, to spark your ideas and creativity.

Conservative	Funny	Impulsive
Liberal	Environmentally	Arrogant
Contemporary	conscious	Bold
Traditional	Adventurous	Brave
Frustrated	Cautious	Caring
Content	Glamorous	Charitable
Outraged	Shy	Choice-oriented
Extroverted	Friendly	On the inside track
Self-important	Wary	Impatient
Youthful	Jaded	Stuck
Young at heart	Class-oriented	Worried
Charismatic	Religious	Ashamed
Closed-off	Spiritual	Civic-minded
Secular-minded	Introverted	Dynamic
Energetic	Community-oriented	Meticulous
Republican	Selfish	Disciplined
Democrat	Money-oriented	Kitschy
Independent	Ambitious	Sexual
Political	Lonely	Raunchy
Stylish	Tired	Inarticulate
Hip	Depressed	Showy
Conventional	Anxious	Cultivated
Fun	Health-conscious	Posh
Concerned	Trendy	Uninhibited
Sophisticated	Proactive	Modest
Educated	Inactive	Powerful
Intellectual	Dull	Angry
Peer-oriented	Proud	Selfless

Plan-oriented	*Fearful*	*Artistic*
Loyal	*Strong*	*Hospitable*
Punctual	*Sheltered*	*Hopeful*
Organized	*Worldly*	*Lost*
Hyper	*Open*	*Overwhelmed*
Tidy	*Progressive*	*Dissatisfied*

2. Now take your list, and choose the attitudes and personality of the people or businesses you work with best. For example, you may have a knack for dealing with anxious people who are a little lost, or you may have a good rapport with artistic individuals who are worldly and open-minded, or you may enjoy working with powerful organizations that are dissatisfied with their current situation and that are plan-oriented.

3. Now refine the list further by choosing the five words or phrases that resonate with you the most. Some of the traits on your list may fit the psychographic of your ideal customer better than others. What you want is the best, most accurate description. Think of this as having to describe your best friend in just five words. You would want to choose the perfect words, not almost perfect words. For example, you may have chosen *showy* and *posh* to describe your ideal customer, but when you have to narrow it down to just five words, you realize that the word *posh* does a better job of describing your customer accurately.

4. Next, you're going to identify the ambitions, hopes, and desires of the customers you love and the customers you would love to have. Again, use the following list as a starting point, and jot down any other words, phrases, or ideas that come to mind as you go through the list.

Safety	*Health*	*Freedom*
Wealth	*Beauty*	*Education*
Friendship	*Youth*	*Career*
Respect	*Abundance*	*Family*
Admiration	*Marriage*	*Children*
Security	*Love*	*Romance*
Free time	*Peace of mind*	*Accolades*

Attention	*Authority*	*Fun*
Status	*Control*	*Truth*
Celebrity	*Guidance*	*Entertainment*
Quiet	*Power*	*Escape*
Enlightenment	*Simplicity*	*Rebirth*
Inspiration	*Adventure*	*Efficiency*
Strength	*Relaxation*	*Deals*
Stuff	*Energy*	*Change*

5. Now take your list and narrow it down to the five aspirations and desires that your customer values most as they pertain to your offering or brand. If you can, put them in order of importance. Which aspirations do you wish to satisfy for your demographic? For example, Virgin Atlantic's customers could embody the values and/or aspirations of an independent spirit, or excitement. Polo Ralph Lauren's customers may aspire to be recognized as refined. Apple's customers may value being understood as being creative, independent, and smart.

6. Now look at both lists and identify which psychographics best fit the type and nature of the products and services you sell.

7. Using your culled list of words, fill in the blanks:

In the Words of Your Customer . . .

Finally a(n) _____ company designed for me. It understands my need for _____ (privacy, freedom, certainty, independence, economy, quality, fun—you name it). It respects my _____ (time, views, beliefs—you name it). It cares about _____ (the environment, helping me learn, discipline—you name it). It knows that _____, _____, and _____ are important to me.

CHAPTER 7

Putting It All Together

Before you take the final step in defining your superniche, let's look at an example of a company that successfully identified an authentic superniche. One of my clients sells an herbal erectile dysfunction tablet. Early on, this company decided that its market is much younger and much more hip than that of Viagra. Looking at the funnel that is its superniche, my client's demographic is single or married men between the ages of 20 and 49, with an annual income of $30,000 to $60,000. My client also added the following distinctions to the demographic profile of its superniche: customers with a high school education and some college who live in the United States and are Internet-savvy.

Moving on to the narrow end of the superniche funnel (the psychographic), my client determined that its erectile dysfunction tablet is for men who want to feel sexier, men who want to see themselves as daring and who want to be better in bed. And here's where the psychographic profile became even more specific: Not only do the members of the company's superniche want to be better in bed, but they also *want their peers to believe* they are better in bed than others in their circle; they want to inspire other men to also become more daring, sexually proficient, and assertive.

Here's the complete description of my client's superniche:

Internet-savvy men (and women who buy for men) who are single or married and live in the United States, are between the ages of 20 and 49, have an income of $30,000 to $60,000, and have completed high school and some college; men with a desire to feel youthful, have more fun, be more daring and sexy, and perform better in bed, who also wish to serve as role models for other men, inspiring them to want the same things.

Notice how the psychographic profile is not about dysfunction at all, even though the product does work for people with erectile dysfunction. Just like the old Oldsmobile campaign that said, "Not your Dad's Oldsmobile," this is not your Dad's erectile dysfunction pill. It's for people who want even better function, to be stronger, hotter, and better in bed. Likewise, the psychographic profile is not at all focused on appealing to the married, average—even, dare I say, boring—couples that other pharmaceutical companies use to represent their target market. My client is aiming at a market that is more exciting, daring, and fun.

Do you see how the demographic and psychographic of my client's specific market came together in one powerful superniche? Do you also see that it will be much easier for my client to tap into the story of its customers' lives, knowing that it does not have to market to *all men on Earth*?

The superniche description just given is succinct, but it is by no means comprehensive. To really pull this off, to find the magic buttons that will motivate the people in your superniche to do business with you, knowing them inside and out is essential. You must know the people in your superniche so well that you can make instinctive decisions about what they might like or dislike and how they might react to information. This next exercise will help you realize that you already know a great deal about your superniche.

Exercise: Pitch the Niche

Not only do you have to know your superniche really, really well, but you also have to be able to describe it accurately and quickly.

While you might be able to fully describe your specific market over a five-course meal, the reality is that you often have mere seconds. Yes, seconds. In retail you have 1.4 seconds, and on your web site you have 13.6 seconds to communicate the essence of your brand.

It takes practice to develop, but if you can Pitch the Niche succinctly and dynamically, people will listen. People will listen because your description is clear and concise, and it speaks to your knowledge of and confidence in your brand. When you fumble around for the words to describe your business, you miss out on an opportunity to connect and inspire.

Learning to Pitch the Niche helps you gain confidence, which translates into a confident brand identity. This, in turn, helps you communicate effectively with customers and vendors. Don't think of this as a sales pitch; think of it as building your *own* confidence in your *own* brand.

So how do you cull your list of demographic and psychographic elements and rearrange them into a great niche pitch? Here is a fill-in-the-blanks script to help you get started. Imagine that you are on *Oprah*. She's going to interview you about your business, namely, your clients. And hey, this is *Oprah*, so you'd better be on your game! Just fill in the blanks on a separate sheet of paper, or download the Oprah script from my web site, www.WorldFamous Company.com.

Oprah: Welcome, [your name]. I'm excited to have you on my show today because when I first heard about your [product or service], I was blown away. And of course, I'm not the only one. Has anyone seen this clip? The one with the mile-long line of people waiting for [your product or service]? Amazing, right?

Audience cheers and applauds.

Oprah: So tell me, who are those people that waited in the rain and the cold for three solid days just to get their hands on your [product or service]?

You: Well, Oprah, I'm delighted to be here because, well, you're Oprah . . .

Audience laughs.

You: But also because I'm so thrilled to share the stories of our customers with you. More than anything, our customers want to feel [safe, appreciated, smart, etc.]. They value [integrity, warmth, efficiency, etc.] and [friendship, peace of mind, family, etc.] over everything else, and that is what we're all about. Frustrated with their experiences with [your competitors], our customers want to be [celebrated, validated, inspired, etc.]. They love the fact that our [product or service] fulfills their need for [support, community, expert advice, etc.].

Audience applauds.

Oprah: Well I guess I'm one of them, because that's what your [product or service] did for me! You know, what really sold me on your brand was that it truly inspired me to [start over, call my mom, go green, etc.].

Audience nods in agreement.

You: Thank you, Oprah. Our customers feel the same way. They prefer [reliability, beauty, discounts, etc.] over [VIP treatment, hard sells, super fast service, etc.], and they love to feel [pampered, loved, respected, etc.]. Our [product or service] gives them exactly that.

Oprah: Thanks for being here. Audience, you're all going home with your very own [product or service], courtesy of [you]!

Audience cheers, applauds, and then faints out of joy and excitement!

To further help you Pitch the Niche, let's imagine that Richard Branson is on Oprah, discussing his new airline, Virgin America. Here's a taste of what he *might* say to Oprah:

> *Our customers want to enjoy the journey as much as the destination. Our customers want to be in command; they want to be able to order the movie they want when they feel like it, not when the airline feels like showing it. Our customers*

want to be able to order their food when they want it, not when the airline says they can be fed. Our customers want to feel that they are special. They're frustrated with feeling that air travel is a chore, and they want to feel that flying is fun again.

Practice Pitching the Niche with your nearest and dearest. If you have a staff, have its members do the exercise on their own, and then combine the best of each pitch into the most inspiring pitch in the history of the world. Get your pitch right, and then practice it until you know it forward and backward. When you know your market and how you are stimulating it, its needs, values, and aspirations become the cornerstone of your brand identity. Business gets more exciting when you understand what specific values and aspirations you are seeking to satisfy in your customers. I actually get giddy when I figure it out because I know I have discovered a way to connect with my superniche. When people "get" what you stand for, they love buying from you. And when you know your niche so well that you can pitch it to anyone—even Oprah—what you stand for will be as clear as day.

The Power of the Superniche

What type of person owns an iPhone? How about a 26-year-old graphic designer living in a hip neighborhood of a major city? Not only does he have an iPhone, but he probably stood in line for an hour to get it, because the iPhone represents an ideal, and owning one screams, "I'm tech-savvy, I value speed and access, and I'm willing to throw down $500 for a first-generation gadget just to prove all of the above."

The ideal customer for iPhone, Polo Ralph Lauren, Virgin Atlantic, Amazon.com, Target, and Wal-Mart is easy to imagine. You could probably even list at least 10 attributes of the superniche for each of these products in less than five minutes. That's how well we know these brands, these *World Famous* brands.

For your business to join the ranks of World Famous brands, you must abandon your desire to sell to a broad, undefined market. Marketing to everyone is marketing to no one because your brand must resonate with consumers on an emotional level, and that can be achieved only through knowing your specific market very, very well.

It's natural to resist tightening your market focus. I realize that at first it seems as though you are limiting your profit potential, but if you have a specific, clearly defined marketplace, you are better equipped to inspire people to do business with you.

Many people convince themselves that they don't know the first thing about inspiring anyone, but we all inspire one another on a daily basis. You may have inspired your friends to go out with you even when they've had a long day. You may have inspired your parents to send you some rainy-day cash. Or you may have inspired your boss to give you a raise, your dog to stay off the furniture, or your spouse to get out of bed and get you your favorite ice cream.

Do you see how you routinely inspire people to take specific actions? If you can do it with your circle, you can do it with your marketplace.

When a company fails to identify and commit to a superniche, it cannot grow. All companies, even the giants of industry, have limited resources. When you attempt to market to a broad group of people and/or businesses, you spread your resources too thin to be effective with any subgroup.

Identifying your superniche, that group of people who would most want to do business with you, allows you to focus your energy, time, and money on a specific group that you know very well. Even superstores have a superniche, albeit a very large one. And you can have a large superniche too, as long as it is tightly defined.

When what you do or what you sell fits into the story of your customers' lives, you inspire them to do business with you. Branding is about providing a space where your customers or clients can be authentic, a place that fits their aspirations as much as it fits their current feelings and circumstances. World Famous brands give their marketplace a voice by empowering people to be exactly who they want to be. When your energies are focused on a superniche rather than on a broad and varied market, you are better able to empower and inspire your marketplace.

Your superniche is made up of the measurable characteristics that are your customers' demographic and the aspirations, feelings, and frustrations that are your customers' psychographic. Think of it as a funnel, with the wide end of the funnel representing the demographic of your superniche and the narrowing of the funnel representing the psychographic of your superniche.

In choosing a demographic, I urge you to think about the type of customers or clients that you love to work with. When you enjoy working with your marketplace, you can fully express your passion for your business, reaching out to touch the hearts and minds of the people in your superniche/market.

Psychographics are wildly important because they speak to the story of your customers' lives. When a business aligns with its customers' story, the way its customers see themselves and who they hope to be, this can compel its superniche not only to do business with it, but also to become devout fans of the brand.

Once you have your superniche clearly defined, you can learn to Pitch the Niche. Often you have only a few seconds to communicate with your marketplace, and you must practice your pitch until it is succinct, dynamic, and effortless. You never know when Oprah will call, or when the next opportunity will come up for you to pitch your World Famous brand!

Exercise: Building Your Brand Profile

Building a brand profile is not complicated, but it does require an open mind and the ability to make decisions.* You might be surprised to learn that the brand profiles I create for my clients are not long at all, maybe a few pages. This, of course, is not a function of the time required to create the profile, but rather reflects the goal of creating a succinct, specific, powerful brand identity. If you can't profile your brand in just 10 pages, you don't know your brand and you don't know your market.

You'll have the opportunity to build your complete brand profile as you work the five steps to creating a World Famous brand. Success stories are the best examples. As I mentioned earlier, throughout the book and the profile-building exercises, I will refer back to two of the most successful brands in the world, Polo Ralph Lauren and Virgin Atlantic. Let's get started!

*Download your free brand profile document at www.WorldFamousCompany.com, press the BRAND PROFILE tab, and enter code WF001.

1. The first step in building a brand profile is to describe the nature of your business, the brand overview. Keep it short and sweet (surprise, surprise), and stick to the facts. If you were Ralph Lauren, you might say something like this:

Polo Ralph Lauren is a lifestyle brand that defines American luxury. Lines offered include sportswear, denim, and tailored clothing for men and women, as well as clothing for infants and children. Polo Ralph Lauren also offers a fragrance line, as well as home furnishings and accessories. Ralph Lauren is sold at Ralph Lauren stores, fine department stores, and on-line retailers.

And if you were Richard Branson, you might say this:

An American subsidiary of Virgin Atlantic, Virgin America is an innovative discount airline that offers passengers an alternative flying experience. Cabins are spacious and feature pleasant mood lighting and wider seats. Passengers are offered a wide array of unique amenities and privileges, such as individual entertainment systems and food and beverages on demand. With a hub in San Francisco, Virgin America flies to five major cities and plans to expand to thirty cities within five years.

2. Once you have completed your brand overview, it's time to describe your superniche. First, describe the demographics from your short list. Then, describe the psychographics from your short list. For example, if you were Ralph Lauren, you might describe your superniche as follows:

Polo Ralph Lauren Demographics

Market: Global

Professionals

People of wealth and leisure

People from affluent communities

People with multiple residences

People who sail, ride horses, and participate in sports such as rugby and polo

Polo Ralph Lauren Psychographics

Wants: Prestige, glamour, luxury, privilege

Values: Quality, exclusivity, style, fine living

Aspires to be: Respected, admired, wealthy, and worldly and sophisticated

And if you were Richard Branson, you might include the following in the description of your superniche:

Virgin America Demographics

Market: United States

Business travelers

Travelers under the age of 50

Travelers from urban centers

Professionals

Virgin America Psychographics

Wants: Space, control, fun

Values: Freedom, innovation, choices

Aspires to be: Cool, cutting-edge, sophisticated, maverick, and respected

Now that you have completed the first two steps in building your brand profile, feel free to set it aside until you have completed Step 3. Or, if you are short on time, feel free to read the summary for Step 3 and continue to build your profile.

Now you know that Ralph Lauren customers are buying not just a shirt, but also a feeling of sophistication and an upper-crust lifestyle. You also know that your customers are not just buying your products or services; they are buying an idea and an experience.

Do you realize how powerful it is to know what you now know? You know which buttons you will be pushing to stimulate your niche. Knowing what is really important to your customers is a gift, so it's time to celebrate. Put down this book right now and sing, scream, or even break open a bottle of Cristal Champagne. Congratulations.

STEP
3

Define Your
Difference

"America is not just a country, it's an idea."

—BONO OF U2

From the first pilgrims who set sail from England in search of religious freedom to the revolutionaries who declared their independence and created a democracy, America has always been more than just a country—it has been an idea. The idea of America is so strong that it compels people to give up their home and their country in order to become an American. It did for me.

Just like my adopted country, your business must represent more than the products or services it sells; it must be perceived as an idea. And that idea must be powerful enough to allow your superniche to live vicariously through it—an idea so profound that it acts as a touchstone for your marketplace.

That sounds like a tall order, I know. But why would you do anything if you don't fully intend to be truly great at it? Why pursue anything if in the process it does not lead you to your higher purpose, to your higher self? Why take the time to develop a brand and build a business if you don't expect it to become World Famous?

Traditionally, business has been about the bottom line, profits, and everything this is done to secure the income you have and create even more income in the future. Rarely do you hear talk about a higher purpose in the boardroom. So if you're feeling uncomfortable with this line of thinking, I understand. You may not be used to it. It takes a major shift in perception to think of your brand as an idea, and a powerful one at that.

Yet this is exactly what you want your customers to do. You want your customers to believe in your brand so much that it is the only possible choice. How can you expect your marketplace to have faith in your business if you cannot rise to this challenge within your own organization?

If you've been reading this book straight through, you've already learned why following the status quo and focusing on a broad market are the kiss of death for most companies, and yet many companies continue to operate using the same methodology, hoping (all the way to bankruptcy court) that their brand catches on. By now you know for sure that wildly successful branding requires daring, authenticity, and a love of your superniche.

I want to stop right now and tell you something vitally important: The fact that you know these truths sets you apart from other businesses. It differentiates you. Even if you never consciously act on this knowledge, the mere fact that you have learned it will influence your decision making and elevate your brand identity to something that holds meaning for your customers. Now it's time to take that knowledge to the next level and build your World Famous brand. And that next level is differentiation.

Let me ask you a question: If the people in your superniche cannot tell the difference between your brand and a competing brand, why would they choose you? If the marketplace cannot distinguish your business from a host of others, how will you stand out as the only choice?

Don't get me wrong. I'm not talking about being different just for the sake of being different or trying to "be the best." I'm referring to defining your authentic brand identity, the essence of your business. In going through this process, you will learn how to differentiate your brand effectively so that in the hearts and minds of your superniche, *you* are the only choice.

Differentiation is a key factor in building your successful brand identity. It's simple logic, really. Why would a consumer choose your business over another? In other words, what is different about your business, what sets it apart? How is your product or service different from that offered by the guys down the street? You may have been asked this question before, perhaps by a potential client, a reporter, or an investor. What was your answer?

Our instincts are to answer these questions based on features and benefits, to compare apples to apples. I want you to shift your focus from product comparisons to brand identity. So, rather than looking at how your product or service is different from the competition, focus on what the essence of your business is. Let others draw comparisons while you stand firmly in your authentic self. When you are clear about your business and your brand identity, your superniche will see that you are different and pick you out from the pack.

Brand differentiation is a simple, yet powerful process of first determining which industry your business truly operates in, and then developing a three-word persona that describes the essence of your brand. This differentiation process can be used for any type or size of business, and it works every time.

By the end of Step 3, you will have a solid brand identity that represents a powerful idea. When your brand is perceived as an idea rather than just "the best," people will be compelled to do business with you. Just as thousands of immigrants saw America as the only place where they could achieve their dreams, your brand will stand out as the only choice.

For more information and to download your free brand profile document, go to www.WorldFamousCompany.com, press the BRAND PROFILE tab, and enter code WF001.

CHAPTER 8

What Business Are You *Really* In?

"Know thyself."

—INSCRIBED ON THE ORACLE SHRINE OF APOLLO, SIXTH CENTURY B.C.

Remember my dare story from Step 1, the one about my first business selling antiques in people's living rooms? And do you also remember another big dare, when I found out *why* Patti at Macy's chose our company, then London Antique Emporium, over the dominant Vintage, Inc.? Well, there's a second act, a period in which, despite all evidence to the contrary (a.k.a. the inventory in my garage), I learned that I wasn't in the antique business at all. And, as in all great stories, there is also a third act—but first things first.

Early on in our business, not long after Patti's first big order, I took an order from John, a different buyer at Macy's. John asked if he would see me at the Visual Merchandising and Store Design (VMSD) trade show in San Diego the following month. Not wanting to seem clueless, I tried to act as if I knew what John was talking about, but he caught on pretty quickly.

"David, you really should be at this show," John said firmly. "Call and see if they have any spaces left. You'll be glad you did."

After thanking John, I did some research on the VMSD show, and things didn't look good. The show was only one month away, there was only one space left in the show, and we had very limited funds. Having never shown at a trade convention before, I had no idea what to expect. We weren't prepared, and yet it seemed that in order to compete, to be taken seriously, we had to show up.

I made an on-the-spot decision and signed us up for the last remaining space. With a total budget of $5,000, including travel and hotel expenses, we headed to Home Depot in search of inexpensive supplies for our booth design. We purchased pegboard for our backdrop, thinking that our antiques and other display items were attractive enough to serve as the focal point of our booth. We also hired a graphic designer to make a brochure to hand out, and then I booked a hotel at $17 per night, which the English reservation receptionist assured me, "as one Englishman to another," was a great hotel.

Four short weeks later, my business partner and I took off for the VMSD show in our rented U-Haul. We arrived at the San Diego Convention Center full of nervous excitement and trepidation. Inside, the exhibition hall was a sea of activity. Union workers hung massive company signage above two-story displays. Forklifts moved heavy equipment and giant boxes of merchandise. More workers stood in cherry pickers hanging designer lighting from the rafters. We felt totally out of our league.

Completely intimidated, we found our booth and assembled our simple pegboard walls. As the hours ticked by, our booth started to take shape, and we felt a bit more confident. Other exhibitors stopped by to introduce themselves and admire our wares. People lent us tools, tape, and power cords. Our anxiety was all but gone. I felt like a kid who had been allowed to come to a grown-up party.

Our excitement building, we worked until midnight and then made our way to our hotel. To our horror, we discovered that it was one step above a public shelter. In fact, a San Diego shelter was checking in a busload of homeless people as we arrived. Old and decaying, the hotel reeked of bleach and ammonia.

Needless to say, our bubble had burst. Surely all the other

exhibitors were safely ensconced in clean, comfortable hotel rooms with room service and cable TV. And here we were, stuck in a fleabag hotel and feeling like rank amateurs. Still, we had no choice but to stay, since we had prepaid for the rooms and had no cash left to spend. Exhausted, we slept in our clothes on top of the sheets.

As we walked into the exhibition hall the morning of the show, all my nervousness was gone. This was where we belonged. Our new friends waved hello as we made our way to our booth. I felt like a privileged member of a fabulous new club. Rather than seeing us as outsiders, the other exhibitors treated us as though we had something real and wonderful to offer. And we did.

The trade show started off with a bang. Since we were the new kids on the block, show attendees flocked to our booth. With all of our merchandise displayed, our booth had actually turned out quite nice. The day went by in a blur; we met lots of new clients, wrote nearly $100,000 of business, and even signed up sales representatives to represent us in states all across the country. Not a bad result from one snap decision.

It turned out that we weren't in the antique business at all. We were in the visual merchandising business. It was only three years since I had arrived from England hoping to sell antiques in living rooms all across America. Now, thanks in part to our exposure at the VMSD show, we were doing business all over the country—but in boardrooms, not living rooms. Our new sales reps brought in more business. Our fax machine buzzed with orders, and big juicy checks arrived in the mail weekly. We hired four employees and started paying ourselves a wage—a real wage, not just pizza and a pint.

Exhibiting at the VMSD show taught us that we had been trying to operate in the wrong industry. When we changed our focus from selling antiques in living rooms to supplying antiques and other props to retailers and corporations, our business really took off. Our client list both expanded and became more impressive. Soon we were working with big retailers like Banana Republic, Nordstrom, and even Nike.

One of our clients was Polo Ralph Lauren, the most successful lifestyle brand in the world. In fact, Ralph Lauren *invented* the lifestyle brand.

Like many of our retail clients, Polo Ralph Lauren hired us to provide antiques and props for its California stores. Each season, we received a list from corporate in New York that detailed the items that the company wanted for the displays. We had a reputation for getting it exactly right, for respecting the Polo Ralph Lauren vision and shipping the perfect props to each store.

One evening over cocktails, we heard some higher-ups at Polo Ralph Lauren talking about a problem at the store in Des Moines, Iowa. That year, a large brass horse had been on the list of required items, but when one of the district managers visited the store, she discovered a big brass cow sitting on a table! Even if you don't care much about fashion, I'm sure you can appreciate the fact that cows do not fit the Polo Ralph Lauren brand—even in Iowa.

It's no surprise that the district managers were appalled at the misinterpretation of the Polo Ralph Lauren brand in Des Moines. When the district manager asked why the store had chosen a brass cow, the manager explained that it was all he could find, and that being in the farming belt, he figured that people in Des Moines liked cows.

Cue: a giant lightbulb over my head.

That night, I realized that we could solve our client's problem. We would be the visual police, ensuring that every Ralph Lauren store display fit the brand flawlessly, every time. I organized a meeting with the key decision makers, and days later we were on a plane to New York.

I remember feeling very daring as we walked into the meeting. This was not a little dare; this was the biggest dare to date. We presented our proposal, explaining that we could solve the problem of inconsistent visual branding by providing a matrix of packages for the display merchandise. We told them that rather than sending a list of items to regional buyers, we would provide photos for approval, and then ship all the merchandise to the individual stores.

I closed my presentation saying, "We will guarantee that your brand is perfectly presented everywhere in the world. You'll never have to walk into a store and see a brass cow ever again."

We got the job.

Within six months, we were providing the visual merchandising for five divisions of Polo Ralph Lauren, and within a year we also landed the Polo Japan and Polo Europe accounts. It wasn't just that I dared to raise the bar; we got the job because I realized that we were *not* a visual merchandising company. We were a branding company. To be precise, we were a "visual branding" company, a term I'm quite proud to proclaim as my own.

We began as an antique business, but we became successful only when we realized that we weren't in the antique industry, we were in the visual merchandising industry. Only when we realized that we were actually in the visual branding industry and built our own brand identity did our business become World Famous. It was a journey, a process that revealed itself over time. As we gained confidence in one industry, we were able to recognize our true industry, our true potential, our true highest idea. In reality, we were still selling antiques and vintage items, yet we were positioned in a better way and were completely differentiated in the marketplace, simply because we knew how we wanted to inspire our market.

Your business may not actually be what it seems to be on paper; the sign above your door may say one thing and deliver another. When you realize the business you are actually in, rather than the business you *appear* to be in, you are better able to build a brand that resonates with your superniche. And in my case, realizing that I was in the branding business opened up new doors for our business and allowed us to grow beyond our wildest dreams.

Here's what happened next.

Within six months of our meeting with Polo Ralph Lauren, we landed Polo Europe. We were doing really well. And then, just like that, the shipping companies messed up 14 separate orders—the very first Polo Europe orders. It was a logistical nightmare. Tempers were frayed, to say the least. We were summoned to New York, and

I was very concerned. I had dared us to take on this monumental task, and we had screwed it up.

Wearing my Prada suit, I walked into 650 Madison Avenue with my business partner and prepared to do some fast talking. We were shown into an all-white room with molded Plexiglas furniture. My "we will fix this problem" speech at the ready, I waited for the scolding from the Polo Ralph Lauren team.

"We want to take Polo Sport to a new level, and we would like to know what you recommend."

What? What on earth were these people talking about? We were prepared for a major tongue-lashing, and they seemed to be looking to us for advice about their brand identity. *Looking to us for advice about their brand development.*

"Tell me what you're looking for," I said.

And just like that, we came into our own. By defining our business as a branding company and taking over the visual merchandising for all of Polo Ralph Lauren's stores, we had changed the way Polo Ralph Lauren perceived our company. We were not just another vendor. We differentiated our company from other sellers by defining what business we were *really* in, which in turn provided a solution to Polo Ralph Lauren's problem.

Polo Ralph Lauren viewed us as a company that knew the importance of consistent visual branding, but, more importantly, it viewed us as a company that provided innovative solutions. That is why, when it wanted to redefine the Polo Sport brand, it looked to our company for a solution. Here was one of the most successful brands in the world, and the company was asking *us* for ideas!

For an hour and a half, we listened to the Polo Ralph Lauren reps discuss their concerns and hopes for Polo Sport, and all the while sweat was dripping down my back onto the Plexiglas chair. We had absolutely no idea what to tell these people, but rather than cut and run, I dared myself to follow through with the vision I had for our company.

"You need a well-thought-out plan. We are honored to be part of the solution," I said, to my own amazement (and that of my business partner), adding, "How long do we have?"

We promised to get back to them before the month was up, and when I stood up from my seat, nearly two hours worth of dripping sweat had collected in the seat. It looked as if I had wet my pants. Horrified, I sat back down and did my best to soak it up with my jacket. It was a memorable day in more ways than one.

When we reached the elevators, my business partner whispered, "Don't say anything. They might be bugged!"

Once we were outside, we let out a scream, and then made a beeline for the nearest bookstore. We were playing with the big boys now, and we had a lot of homework to do.

You might be surprised at how many businesses misunderstand what industry they are really in, and consequently are never able to reach their full potential. Had we continued to view our business as an antiques and props company, we might never have become a multimillion-dollar visual branding company. Once we understood what type of business we actually had, we were able to create our own World Famous brand.

I'm not suggesting that you trade selling office supplies for flipping burgers. This isn't about doing a complete 180-degree turn; it's about understanding what your business *provides* to the customer. We didn't just wake up one morning and decide to be a branding business. We *already were* a branding business. We just didn't know it until that lightbulb went on over my head.

Even though we had realized that we were actually in the visual branding industry, not the antiques and props industry, we were still going by the name London Antique. We knew that we needed to rebrand our business. Polo Sport, Nautica, and many of our other clients were not using vintage items any longer. Our brand did not fit our industry, and it did not portray an image that fit the needs of our clients.

This fact became painfully obvious when we landed the Tommy Hilfiger account. We had a $300,000 sample order ready to go, but when the papers came across Tommy Hilfiger's desk, he wanted to cancel it. He did *not* want to do business with an antique company, and with a name like London Antique, what else could we be about? Fortunately, his staff explained who we were, and he finally agreed to complete the order.

Within six weeks, we had rebranded and came up with a new name for our company, Propaganda. We did lots of business with Tommy Hilfiger, even more after we changed our name. Having the right name is really important. Once you know your industry and brand identity, you are much more able to know the right name for your company when you hear it.

You don't need to reinvent your business. You need to *discover* the industry in which your business truly operates.

Look at the leaders of brand identity. Some would say that Polo Ralph Lauren is in the business of selling clothes and home goods. However, Ralph Lauren would say that he is in the lifestyle business. Some would say that Virgin Atlantic is in the airline industry. Richard Branson would say that he is in the entertainment business. Do you see what I mean? This is very important, because such thinking and such ideas open up a world of opportunity.

Imagine that you sell real estate. Are you in the business of selling homes, or are you in the wish fulfillment industry? What if you own a chain of bowling alleys? Are you in the bowling business or the fun business? How about an undertaker? Is he in the funeral business, or would he say that he was in the celebration of life business?

What business are *you* really in?

For example, in my current business, I often speak publicly. People could consider me to be a speaker, but I consider myself to be an "info-tainer."

Exercise: Define Your Industry

All the exercises in this book are connected, and one exercise may inform an earlier exercise. After you complete this exercise and move on in the World Famous brand-building process, you may have a realization (or even a revelation) about your business and the industry in which it operates and want to change or refine your answer. So don't stress or worry over this exercise. You can always modify your answers if something else occurs to you.

Still, I do encourage you to complete this exercise before you move on in the process. Discovering which industry your business truly belongs in will inform everything you do going forward and will make the work you have left to do so much easier. When you decide what business you are in, you open the door to being differentiated.

1. *What ideas does your company represent?*

Remember not to squeeze your brain, and don't be frustrated if you don't have your answer in 20 seconds. Just know it will come.

America represents freedom and unlimited opportunity. You might even say that America is *in the business of* freedom and unlimited opportunity; it's the American brand. Think back to the last time you listened to someone talk about the United States and why she loves living here. Time after time, you will hear people say that America is about freedom and opportunity. They might use slightly different words, but the meaning is the same.

Now think about your company and what it represents to your customers. Try imagining what they would say to a reporter about your company and why they choose to do business with you. Does your business represent financial security? How about wellness? Do your customers view your business as innovative, or even genius?

If you're just starting a company or don't yet have a good handle on how your business is perceived by your customer base, make a list of the idea(s) that you *would like* your business to represent. This is a great exercise even if you are pretty clear about how your business is perceived, because it speaks to a higher purpose, the vision you have for your business and your brand.

Once you come up with a few ideas, move on to the next question. Too many ideas will confuse the issue, making this exercise labor-intensive. And we can't have that now, can we?

2. *How do those ideas relate to your industry?*

Your short list of ideas is actually a list of clues to help you determine what industry your business operates in. For example, imagine you own and operate a bed-and-breakfast inn located in a popular seaside village. You might initially view your business as being hospitality and tourism. Yet after brainstorming, you realize that the ideas your B&B represents to your customers are escape, relaxation, and romance. Looking at this list of ideas, you might determine that you are actually in the romance industry (since escape and relaxation are part of what makes romance possible). Who knew, right?

Stop and think about this for a few seconds. Now that you know you are in the romance industry, how will that affect your ability to differentiate your brand identity from the countless B&Bs in your quaint little town? It's huge, really. Transformational. Revolutionary. (Champagne, anyone?)

All this time you've been fighting for the same tourists using very similar marketing techniques, but now you realize that you're not in the same industry at all. What a relief! Now you can get down to business and define your brand as the only choice in your industry. You can attract customers from all over the region, the country, even the world, just by focusing on romance. Your marketing efforts will be more effective. Your customer service will align with your true mission. You may even discover new product lines that are now a natural fit with your industry.

Knowing your *true* industry allows you to break from the pack and forge your own path, an action that, on its own, differentiates you from your competitors.

See how you did that? Pretty slick, right?

3. *What are the ultimate benefits to your customer?*

Note: If you have already come up with your industry, you can skip this question. It's designed to help you come up with the same answer using a different route.

What are the benefits of your product or service? Recall that I mentioned that differentiating your brand is not about describing the literal features or benefits of your products or services, and it certainly is not about comparing how your products or services stack up against the competition. What I'm suggesting here is that you consider the ultimate benefit your customers receive, which is more experience-based, more values-based, and more aspiration-based.

Again, go with your gut; list just a few benefits, and move on to defining the industry in which your business operates. You might be surprised!

When you discover the business you are truly in, you might determine that you need a new superniche, or you may find a better one to focus on. How does your superniche fit with your true industry?

CHAPTER 9

What Are the Personality, Attitude, and Values of Your Brand Identity?

"Some people say they haven't yet found themselves. But the self is not something one finds; it is something one creates."

—THOMAS SZASZ, 1920–, AMERICAN PSYCHIATRIST

We called it the Party Room.

It had sandblasted brick walls, mosaic-tiled pillars, a dance floor, and a disco ball. It was outfitted with the latest gizmos and gadgets; a coffee table came up from the middle of the dance floor, and a 13-foot movie screen dropped from the ceiling. Beanbags were the only seating—even for the suits from the bank. It was the Propaganda boardroom, and anyone who ever met with us in that room will never forget it—least of all the suits. In fact, it was in doing business with our bankers *in* the Party Room that our beliefs about brand differentiation were put to the test.

Things were going well for Propaganda, and we wanted to parlay that success into even greater success by expanding the business. We needed a bump in our line of credit. We already had a

$750,000 line of credit with Citibank, and since we were a good account, the branch manager agreed to meet with us to discuss our request for a jump to a $1.5 million line of credit. When the branch manager showed up at our office, he also brought the area manager, the regional manager, and four or five minions. Fortunately, my CFO had given me a list of key words that bankers like to hear.

I gave them a tour of the office, starting at the Zen Room, a clean and crisp room with only chalkboards and stools. I used the banker-speak I had memorized, and as I showed them around, they seemed genuinely impressed with our business—until I opened the door to the Party Room. The antithesis of the Zen Room, the Party Room, with its disco ball, silk drapes, dance floor, and giant bar, clearly made an impression on the suits. To say they were shocked would be an understatement.

When we sat down on beanbags to conduct our meeting, I noticed that the regional manager had his arms folded across his chest. His whole demeanor had changed, and I knew that he was beyond uncomfortable—he was annoyed. I realized I couldn't stick to the script.

"Have any of you ever been in a room like this?"

An emphatic "no" reverberated in the room. I turned to the regional manager and asked, "Will you ever forget this room?"

"Never," he replied sternly.

"*That* is why you should give us the loan—because you will never forget this room," I explained. "We understand differentiation."

Within two weeks we had a $1.5 million line of credit.

For a company that provided innovative visual branding and brand identity packages to some of the world's best-known companies, Propaganda's boardroom had to be something totally different from the norm. The Party Room was 100 percent fun, 100 percent memorable, and 100 percent in line with our business personality. It was totally unique, differentiated from any other boardroom *on the planet*. The cost of our successful brand differentiation? Only cents on the dollar compared to the standard everyday mahogany bored—oops, I mean *board*room.

Like it or not, your business has a personality. Whether it's stodgy, precious, hip, or traditional, your business has a personality that serves as a *major* component of your brand identity. Every business has a personality; it's just that most of these personalities are boring or underutilized. This goes back to the problem with sticking to the status quo: Trying to fit in just leads to blending in. And when you blend in with all the rest, how can your customers differentiate you from your competitors? For that matter, how can they see you at all?

What draws you to people? What compels you to introduce yourself to someone you see across a crowded room? What inspires you to take the leap and make a connection with someone you've just met? Do you prefer to spend time with the wallflowers or with the people who are telling great stories? On a first date, would you ditch a perfect match if he bored you to tears? On the flip side, would you consider a second date or more if your polar opposite had an intriguing personality and a fantastic attitude toward life?

Just as personality is a make-or-break factor in personal relationships, the personality of your brand identity is a major component in your relationship with your marketplace. Your brand personality (or lack thereof) directly affects how—and if—your marketplace chooses to do business with you.

All businesses have a personality that is unique to them, and a great many of them are total duds. Boring, boring, boring. Most businesses don't have a clue what their personality is or how to use it to engage their marketplace because they are focused primarily on selling. Other businesses choose to have a boring personality because of their fear of standing out. (Remember, you already know that being authentic and daring to stand out are essential to building a World Famous brand, so just by knowing and agreeing with this principle, you are well on you way to cultivating a compelling business personality.)

Dictionary.com Unabridged defines personality as "the visible aspect of one's character as it impresses others." The key words I want you to focus on in that definition are *visible* and *impresses*. The personality of your business is what is visible to your marketplace and makes an impression on them, which, in turn, inspires them to do business with you.

You have to have a specific business personality. You cannot just set up shop and hope that people will come. Many people in branding will tell you that you must have an icon, a logo, and a corporate identity (i.e., brochures, business cards, and so on). While you may very well need these things, they are not the place to start building your brand identity. Before you can go about creating a logo and stationery, you must first know *the personality of your company.*

Your business has to have meaning; it has to resonate with your marketplace, or you will fade into obscurity. Think of it in the context of reality television. Whether you are competing for a singing contract or someone's heart, personality will make or break you. Not having a personality makes you forgettable, so you're cut in the first round. Giving out mixed messages that show that you aren't sure who you are means that you won't make it to the finals. And presenting an inauthentic personality based on calculation rather than heart means that not only will you be cut, but you'll be the butt of every joke.

Creating a brand identity is about building a solid relationship with your superniche. Brand identities have human elements to them—attitude, personality, and values among them. Humanize your brand so that you can enjoy a meaningful relationship with your customers. Dare to cultivate a powerful, genuine personality and express that personality in all aspects of your business. Dare to stand out. Dare to differentiate your brand. Dare to engage your marketplace in a meaningful relationship that inspires raving, loyal fans.

Branding is about showing up. When a business fails to give consideration to its personality, it doesn't show up. Sure, its products and services are there for the purchasing, but where is the heart and soul of that business? Where is the fire? Where is the dream? Where is the vision? Where is that "thing" that customers relate to and come back to for more?

Some businesses are built on the personality of the founder or CEO, such as Polo Ralph Lauren or Virgin Atlantic. Other businesses cultivate a personality separate from those of the founders, such as Starbucks or Volkswagen. But they all show up. They all have a clearly defined personality that resonates with their superniche and is totally reliable. It's this level of personality that allows people to identify with a brand because it fits into the story of their lives.

When you are cultivating a business personality, I urge you to focus a great deal on attitude. While attitude may not be *everything*, it's hugely significant. Think about it in terms of your own life. What was the quality of your life when you took on the attitude that you could do or be anything? Better, right? Great, even?

(I know you've had this attitude about life once or twice because you, dear reader, are my superniche. While you may also have had feelings of despair or hopelessness, I know that you have also felt that you could do the impossible. Otherwise, you wouldn't be reading a book on creating a World Famous brand!)

The attitude of your business is part of its brand identity. While the personality of your business may be cutting-edge, for example, the attitude is how that personality is expressed. A poor attitude can tank your brand, and a positive attitude can elevate it beyond your wildest dreams.

Like many aspects of branding, defining your business personality can feel a bit mysterious, as if your personality had to be dreamed up by a team of marketing savants. Some of you may feel a bit nervous about defining your personality for fear of choosing the "wrong" one. Let me tell you, you are the best person for this job. You already *know* your business personality; you just need to know how to clarify it and refine it so that it becomes a powerful branding tool.

In many ways, my job as a brand identity specialist is to help my clients discover what they already know to be true. You know who you are and what your business is all about. You can do this.

In the next few chapters, you're going to define your brand personality using just three words. Yes, only three. But first try this personality exercise so that I can prove to you that you know more about your business than you realize.

Exercise: Boardroom Design

Designing a boardroom for your business is a great exercise because it reveals how much you actually do know about your brand personality—and because it's fun!

What Are the Personality, Attitude, and Values of Your Brand Identity?

If you don't have a boardroom or a conference room in your office, or if you don't have an office at all, just imagine the space and how you would design it to reflect the personality of your brand. For questions 1 through 3, choose a public area of your office for evaluation. If your office is a home office, think about where you meet clients. Is it at a local coffee shop or restaurant? If you conduct most of your business online and never meet your clients in person, consider how your web site or general online presence reflects the personality of your business.

1. If you have a boardroom or a conference room, describe what it looks like in detail. Does it have a glass, metal, or wood table? Are there windows in the room? Do you have curtains, shades, blinds, or nothing at all? What type of chairs do you have in the room? Is there any technology in the room? Be as specific as possible.

2. What does your boardroom reveal about the personality of your business? Imagine that you are walking into your boardroom for the first time. What would your initial impressions be?

3. Do you feel that your boardroom best represents the personality of your business? If so, why do you feel that way? Be as specific as possible.

4. If you could start over from scratch and get the boardroom of your dreams, how would you design the room to reflect your company's personality?

5. What would you call your boardroom?

6. In what ways would your boardroom be different from other boardrooms?

7. How could you use your boardroom to effectively communicate the personality of your business?

CHAPTER 10

Hip, Young Gunslingers and Rude, Obnoxious Anarchists—Three Essential, Powerful, Earth-Shattering Words

WANTED: HIP, YOUNG GUNSLINGERS

In an effort to ditch the belief that it was out of touch with new trends, the *New Musical Express* posted an ad for new writers. It was 1976, and the British weekly magazine desperately needed a turnaround. Sales were down, and the dwindling readership sneered at the publication, viewing it as being caught up in the stodgy and stagnant mainstream music scene of the mid-seventies.

Now the stuff of legend, the ad got the attention of Tony Parsons and Julie Burchill, a pair of smart, cynical, and funny writers. Three simple yet powerful words—*hip, young gunslingers*—had landed the two writers that could transform the magazine and save it from imminent failure. Within a few short months, the *New Musical Express* had regained its status as the must-read of youth culture and became number one in its market, the obvious choice.

Burchill and Parsons helped to turn things around for the *New Musical Express* by focusing on the burgeoning punk rock scene. One of the most infamous bands to come out of that movement was the Sex Pistols, a group of angst-ridden guys that made punk rock a household name.

Just one year before the *New Musical Express* posted its ad, the Sex Pistols was on the lookout for a new front man, and, like the magazine, the group knew exactly what it wanted:

Rude, Obnoxious Anarchist

In a country steeped in royal tradition, class boundaries, and a conservative BBC controlling most mainstream television and radio, there was no voice representing poor working-class youth—that is, until the Sex Pistols came on the scene. The new front man had to represent working-class youth; he had to give it a voice. He had to be a rude, obnoxious anarchist who could embody everything the disillusioned kids were feeling.

Who did the Sex Pistols find to step into this role? None other than Johnny Rotten, a talented, sneering, angry musician who had the look and the attitude that the band wanted. And why did Johnny accept the offer to join the band? Because it was a group of rude, obnoxious anarchists, that's why—just like him. With Johnny Rotten on board, the band easily landed the manager it had been courting: Malcolm McLaren, who had been on the lookout for a group of "sexy, young assassins" since 1973.

The rest, as they say, is history. The Sex Pistols became one of the most famous bands in history. Even the BBC eventually declared it, "the definitive English punk rock band." Definitive. The only choice. That's quite a feat for a ragtag group of punks with more attitude than cash, more confidence than clout.

The Sex Pistols first developed a personality that appealed to the poor, disenfranchised youth of Britain, and then came to epitomize rebellion for a far wider audience. The Sex Pistols was exciting and a bit dangerous. Soon, anyone who ever felt the desire to rebel against the norm could relate to the band. Anyone who ever felt fed up or frustrated could identify with it. Anyone who ever wished she could behave badly, break from tradition, and tell someone to "piss off" was drawn to the Sex Pistols and all that it represented. Eventually, the band inspired *masses of people* to buy into its brand.

The Sex Pistols spoke to—and on behalf of—a large audience that transcended class, gender, and geography. The band audaciously dared to do and say what most people could only dream of, and it didn't care what anyone thought or said about it. The rude, obnoxious, anarchistic persona went beyond the stage, as the members' public trysts made headlines.

The Sex Pistols was the new voice of inspiration for an entire generation. Its message of "rebel, dare to be yourself, go for it" ignited a fire in its fans, making the band and the individual members World Famous.

Hip, Young Gunslingers
Rude, Obnoxious Anarchist
Sexy, Young Assassins

The Sex Pistols defined punk rock music, influencing other World Famous bands such as Green Day, Guns N' Roses, Nirvana, and The Clash, and was inducted into the Rock and Roll Hall of Fame in 2006.

The *New Musical Express* is the definitive source for rock and roll music news in Britain and has championed new musicians since its famous 1976 turnaround. Now simply referred to as *NME*, today this once-stagnant magazine extends its influence through an eponymous radio program, television program, music festivals, and a music awards show.

All of this success from choosing three good words? Absolutely. The more clearly and precisely you can define your business, your core values, and your personality, the more clearly and precisely you can stand out from the crowd. It's a foundation stone in the process of creating a World Famous brand.

Significantly, the three words chosen by the Sex Pistols not only authentically expressed what the band was looking for, but also clearly defined the personality of its brand.

What did the media need to know about this upstart band? Its members were rude, obnoxious anarchists. What did the artist designing its album cover need to know? The band members were rude, obnoxious anarchists. What did the audience need to know? They were rude, obnoxious anarchists. Knowing these three defining words made it simple for reporters to review the band's music, for its manager to promote it, and for graphic designers to produce T-shirts and concert posters. And it made thousands of kids choose the Sex Pistols' music over the "popular" music of the day, which in turn *made its music popular.*

The same was true for the *New Musical Express.* "Hip, young gunslingers" communicated everything anyone needed to know about the tone and personality the magazine wanted to engender.

If a group of poorly educated working-class youths in London could define the heartbeat of its band with just three words and go on to become World Famous, *you can too.*

If a failing London tabloid could define its core with just three words as it screamed toward annihilation and go on to become World Famous, *you can too.*

Were the Sex Pistols and the *New Musical Express* masters of business or just lucky? Maybe, maybe not. At the very least, they were aware of *three essential, powerful, earth-shattering words* that described the heart of their business and the foundation of their message. And, if they did it, *you can too.*

In the next few chapters, you will find *three essential, powerful, earth-shattering words* that define the attitude, personality, and values of your brand identity. In choosing these three words, you not only build the foundation of your brand, but also liberate it from the confines of convention and indecision. With these three words, your brand comes alive; it becomes three-dimensional. With these three words, you can make branding and marketing decisions efficiently, speak to your superniche in a way that resonates with it, and effortlessly expand your reach. With these three words, you can move mountains—your business can become World Famous.

CHAPTER 11

Creating Your Own 3-D Brand Identity

The Sex Pistols isn't the only wildly successful brand to utilize three words to become the definitive brand in its marketplace. Look at the brands you love, the brands you admire, and the brands you choose most often. Which three words describe the personality, attitude, and values of these brands? Here are three of my favorites:

Apple: *Imagination. Design. Innovation.*

Aston Martin: *Power. Beauty. Soul.*

Virgin Atlantic: *Rebellious. Champion. Maverick.*

    Are these brands definitive in their marketplace? Are they the only choice? Absolutely. Remember, their marketplace is a tightly defined superniche made up of both demographics and psychographics. And each of these World Famous, powerhouse brands *owns* its superniche.

    Just look at how well they do.

    Imagination. Design. Innovation. When you look at Apple's full range of products, from the iPhone to iTunes to MacBooks, it's easy to see its three words in action. Time after time, Apple releases a new product or a redesign of a product that makes front-page news and compels thousands of people to take off work and stand in line for hours in order to get one. Apple is seen as an imaginative innovator, which is also how its raving fans want to be viewed.

Have you ever visited an Apple Store? If you haven't, find one near you and visit it as soon as possible. Apple's three words are evident in every aspect of its stores, from the hands-on product displays to the Genius Bar designed to help you become an innovator too. Apple Store events are like movie premieres, and the stores regularly feature music performances and parties, reflecting the imaginative, über-cool personality of the brand.

Power. Beauty. Soul. Every one of Aston Martin's cars embodies its three words. People dream of owning an Aston Martin *because* it represents power, beauty, and soul. In owning an Aston Martin—or rather, *driving* an Aston Martin—you *become* powerful, beautiful, and soulful.

The Aston Martin is so cool that it's the *only* car that James Bond will drive. Aston Martin is a company that knows who it is. It knows that it represents power, beauty, and soul. Every aspect of its business supports and reflects the company's three-word, three-dimensional persona—the personality, attitude, and values of the brand.

Andy Wilman, executive producer of *Top Gear*, Britain's highly popular authority on everything car-related, had this to say about Aston Martin:

> *The Best Car in the real world simply has to be Aston Martin. Aston Martins are the only supercars which retain a charm and innocence that makes them cool forever.*

Cool forever. Now that's impressive.

The only supercar. Wouldn't you like to be considered the definitive supercar—or bagel shop, or wedding planner, or pet sitter—*forever?*

Rebellious. Champion. Maverick. By now you know that I *love*

Virgin Atlantic. For daring, adventurous types, Virgin is the only choice. The very first time I flew to the United States, there was only one airline for me. I simply *had* to fly Virgin Atlantic. I had been reading all about Richard Branson's latest business in the newspapers and watching stories about its launch on television, and I had become genuinely excited about his venture.

I loved the way this young, controversial, daring entrepreneur could be so outspoken. Branson made it seem like competing with British Airways was his birthright, and he spoke to those of us who ever felt the need to stand up to stuffy, old-fashioned bureaucracy in any form. Therefore, purely by association, I felt like a maverick. I felt rebellious. I felt that my rights were being championed simply by taking my seat.

Do you see how Apple, Aston Martin, and Virgin Atlantic use their three words to cultivate a World Famous brand? Do you see how each of these companies embodies its three words in every aspect of its business, from product to marketing to the people associated with the brand?

Apple, Aston Martin, and Virgin Atlantic use their three words to stimulate the psychographics of their superniche, compelling their marketplace to do business with them. Think about what it means to be "a Mac person," to drive an Aston Martin, or to fly Virgin Atlantic. The 3-D persona behind each of these brands inspires raving fans because it speaks to the highest version of themselves, the person they aspire to be. The maverick in me. The innovator in the Apple fan. The powerful driver in James Bond.

Now apply the same paradigm to your own company. If you had to choose just three words to describe your business, what it feels like to do business with you, which words would you choose?

Certain. Charming. Unconventional. Those are my words.

My three words describe both my personality and that of my business, because as an author of books and DVDs that guide you through the brand identity process and as a speaker (info-tainer), I am my brand identity. With a business that has its own personality separate from that of its founder or CEO, which is most businesses, the same principles apply. We may not know who is behind Aston Martin, but we sure know the personality of that brand. At Propaganda, our words were *certainty, fun,* and *respect,* and we delivered on all three.

Your three words are the foundation of your brand. They inform and energize every aspect of your business. Use your three words as an acid test to determine if you are staying true to your brand identity. Do your business cards reflect your brand identity? How about your web site? Your voicemail message? Your e-mail signature?

Your three words give you a context from which you can make nearly every business decision. They help you focus by narrowing your field of options to those that fit with your brand personality. Your three words help you articulate your goals and vision with vendors such as graphic designers and web designers. They prevent you from going off on a tangent that does not serve your company, allowing you to devote all your resources to connecting with your superniche. Do you see how useful your three words could be? The 3-D, three-word persona doesn't just show you the path; it *clears the path.*

Once you choose the right three words—and by right, I mean essential, powerful, and earth-shattering—you can begin the process of filling those shoes. Because, and this is really exciting, your three words are also a call to action. Your three words will inspire you to embody them.

I've always found that charm solves more problems than otherwise, and I've never cared for rude people in restaurants, airplanes, or anyplace actually. As they say in Texas, you attract more bees with honey than you do with vinegar. I believe that charm opens doors and cements relationships, and this belief is just part of who I am. Certainty is as important to me as it is to my market. People need certainty, especially when they're embarking on a journey into their own brand identity; they need to know that they are in good hands. And for my third dimension, *unconventional* is inherent. How could anyone specialize in standing out if he was all about being conventional, toeing the line, and fitting in? I can't help but shy away from the status quo; this is part of my DNA, and it represents my values.

Once I defined my brand identity with three words, it gave me *more* certainty; I was *more* charming and *more* unconventional. With my three words set, I was able to turn up the volume on the personality, attitude, and values of my brand identity. Over time, I became an expert on becoming more *authentic.* I *own certain, charming,* and *unconventional.* And once you have chosen your three words, you will own them too.

Your three words are an acid test for your brand personality and a call to action. This is the magic of having three essential, powerful, earth-shattering words—*your* three essential, powerful, earth-shattering words.

When it is thoughtfully done, this process of finding three words is self-fulfilling. As you brainstorm and work to find the three words for your business, you will feel inspired and energized; you may even feel larger than life. By the end of this process, not only will you have your three words, but you will also have a renewed passion for your business and a higher vision of what your business can become.

Why Just Three Words?

By now, with all this talk of three words, you probably have a number of words swirling around in your mind. It may suddenly seem daunting to choose just three from among those that are breaking through your subconscious as you read, watch television, and generally go about your day. After all, they're all good words. You like them. Your friends like them. Why not just use all of them and get even *more* bang for your buck?

Do you remember why you narrowed your marketplace down to a superniche? Because marketing to a broad market is generally ineffective and depletes your resources. This is part of the reason why you must choose only three words to describe the personality, attitude, and values of your brand. A tight and concentrated three-word persona allows you to focus your energy on building your brand around that identity. If you had ten words, or even five words, your energy would be scattered and confused, leaving too much open to interpretation.

Second, you want to present a clear, concise brand identity to your marketplace. More words muddy the waters, leaving a disjointed impression that confuses your superniche. How many times have you chosen not to do business with a company because it "just doesn't seem to know who it is"? Think of it like this: More words are more personalities.

Having three words that describe the three dimensions of your brand allows for ease of communication in the many ways you will be sharing your brand identity with the world. Three dimensions allow for simplicity, so that you can get your message across and make an immediate impact.

A cohesive brand personality made up of just three dimensions allows you to become the definitive business in your marketplace. Just as Aston Martin is the *only supercar*, your brand can secure a position as the only choice in your marketplace. But it is next to impossible to do this if your brand personality is not clear and clearly imparted. How can you expect to be the definitive anything if you haven't dared to succinctly define your business?

If you're feeling concern right about now, don't stress. I understand. Some people wonder, what if I get my words wrong? What if I start organizing my business around the *wrong* three words, the wrong dimensions? What if there is a better word out there, or even *three* better words? These are all very real concerns, and you aren't the first to have them. A client once offered to add an extra $5,000 to my consulting fee if she could "just have one more word"! It was funny at the time, but of course I had to turn her down.

But imagine what would have happened if I had relented and let my bulk-buying client choose ten words instead of three. Can you envision how diluted her brand personality would be with ten words to describe it? After a while, the words would be in competition with one another, rather than being in harmony, and the dimensions would confuse and confound. The meaning behind the brand would become confused, weakening the foundation of the brand and blurring the chance to connect with the hearts and minds of her marketplace.

In rare circumstances, you may find two words that you love and then struggle to find a third. Just in case you are among this minority, let me tell you in advance that the answer is no. Your foundation cannot have just two words. Each word represents a dimension of your three-dimensional brand identity. It must have depth and a degree of complexity that only a third dimension can deliver. Do you want your marketplace to see you as two-dimensional? Do you want it to see you as flat, like a photograph, or as fantastic 3-D, the living and breathing *real thing*?

If you were to choose three words right now to describe the personality, attitude, and values of your business, what would they be? What words have you inadvertently chosen already? Do they fit? Are they the words you would choose? Do they conflict with one another? Do they set your business apart from the crowd? Or do they pull your company into the ruling homogeneous pile that makes up you and your competition?

Choosing just three words to describe the personality, attitude, and values of your business is scary. In my experience working with clients, friends, and colleagues, choosing three words can be the most challenging step in building a brand identity, simply because of the "what ifs": What if I get it wrong? What if my customers don't like my words? What if my staff or colleagues won't get behind my words? What if my business can't live up to my words? I've seen grown adults look petrified during this process. I've seen people run for the hills, or grab their favorite bottle of booze, or throw their hands in the air and shout, "Just tell me what my words are!"

Word anxiety is normal. I see it with every client and in every audience of every seminar. To date, I have yet to meet anyone who did not struggle at least a little with his three words, which is why I developed a failure-proof process to help you discover and select your three essential, powerful, earth-shattering words. I even included exercises to help you test your words, so that you can fend off the word anxiety and feel great about your decision.

So don't worry. While you are the only person who is qualified to truly know the right three words that represent the three dimensions of your brand, here's a great process for you to use. But first, you need to warm up your brain in preparation for the tasks ahead. While you may be tempted to skip the warm-up exercises and move on to the next chapter, I encourage you to stay the course and do them anyway. They don't require much time, and they will start to train your brain to retrieve the type of answers you need to complete the three-word process.

Exercise: Warm-Up

This exercise is designed to get you thinking about descriptive words. As humans, we are constantly describing and labeling things and people so that our brain can sort out the information. So you're an old pro! This exercise will help you remember that, and will build your confidence for the all-important exercises to follow.

Answer the following series of questions with your top-of-mind experience, rather than mind-squeezing, face-grimacing effort. Just list what first comes to mind and move on to the next question. Your brain is about to get a big workout, so keep the warm-up easy and fun. For each of the following questions, try to limit your answer to three words.

Your three words communicate the identity of your brand to all who are involved in expressing it, from graphic designers to sales personnel. With your 3-D, three-word persona, you can screen all of your branding to be certain that every component accurately represents your brand identity.

1. What does it feel like when you sit in your car? The operative word here is *feel*. You're not describing the interior of your car; you're describing what it feels like to be in your car.

2. Think about the last web site you visited. How did it make you feel? Excited? Relieved? Amused?

3. What about the last restaurant you visited? How did you feel while you were eating there? Did you feel relaxed? Frustrated? Important? Invisible? Perhaps you had a meal at a chain restaurant like Olive Garden or Chili's and you felt relaxed, or bored, or comfortable. Or maybe you tried out a new neighborhood café that made you feel anxious, or pampered, or excited.

4. Have you ever been asked to describe yourself in just three words? If so, what would they be? If you only had ten seconds

to do it, could you? Describe yourself in under ten seconds using just three words.

5. What three words would you use to describe the neighbor you know best? You know, the one that picks up your mail while you're on vacation and borrows your tools. What about the neighbor that you know the least about? How would you describe the neighbor that you wave to across the yard, but have never met?

6. Now describe the worst teacher you experienced at school, using just three words.

7. Let's use an example of someone almost everyone reading this book would be familiar with. Let's use Brad Pitt. What three words would you conjure up? I would guess that in describing Brad Pitt, many of you listed some version of these three words: *sexy, handsome*, and *talented.* These words might fit Brad, but how do we know they are specifically about Brad?
Sexy, handsome, and talented could be the description of just about any successful actor—or any man, for that matter. Those three words are simply too vague and homogeneous. So let's list some new words to describe Brad. Try to come up with three words that really set Brad Pitt apart from other actors—words such as *disarming* or *altruistic* or *riveting*, for instance.

8. Now that you see the specificity to aim for, describe Brad's better half, Angelina Jolie, using three words.

9. What about a different icon, someone like Martin Luther King, Jr.? Which three words would you use to describe him?

10. What about Oprah Winfrey? How would you describe her using just three words?

11. Now let's look at your interests, what occupies your time. Describe your favorite television show in three words. Do the same with your favorite hobby and your favorite sports team. If you don't have a hobby and/or don't follow sports, come up with a three-word description for your favorite film and your favorite book. Or, come up with three words to describe all five. You need the practice.

12. Think back to the strangest place you've ever been, and describe it in three words. It could be a city, a room, a building, or even an outdoor spot. Try to use feeling words, and be as specific as possible.

13. Try to remember the first time you fell in love. First, describe the setting in three words. Then, describe the object of your affection in three words. Lastly, describe the feelings you experienced in three words. The goal here isn't to be clever or cute, but to come up with three words that uniquely and honestly describe your experience.

Do you feel warmed up and ready to go? In the next few chapters, you will start the process of discovering and choosing your three words, beginning with creating a master list of active words, any of which could be one of your three essential, powerful, earthshattering words.

I recommend that you keep a notebook handy to jot down words when you're not actively working the exercises. Sometimes words jump out at you from unlikely places. You might find the perfect word on the side of a mayonnaise jar (*fresh*), or on the front of a magazine (*cosmopolitan*), or as you read through tonight's television show listings (*hysterical*), and I don't want you to forget it. Keep the notebook with you when you watch television, when you're at work, and even on the bathroom counter while you take a shower—you never know when you'll come across a new word that could be a slam dunk for your company.

CHAPTER 12

Brainstorming Guidelines—How to Get Your Words

Here are a few guidelines to help you find your three essential, powerful, earth-shattering words. I know, I know; you want to just jump in and get started. Please read through these guidelines first. It will take only a few minutes, and then you'll be better able to discern when a word is worthy of making it onto your brainstorm list and when it is not. Finding your three words is a bit like a treasure hunt, and the following guidelines will help you stay on course.

Guideline 1: Authenticity

Do choose words that are authentic to your business experience. *Don't* waste your time listing words that do not represent your company or your values. The goal here is to come up with a varied list of possible words for your three-word persona. *Don't* try to impress your old business school roommate or the guys who gave you your first bank loan. While you may be tempted to use words that sound "cool" or "smart," that's not the instinct I'm hoping you'll lead off with. When you deliberately go for cool or smart, the result very often looks fake, and sometimes even desperate. But when you start with what feels authentic and honest, it will invariably come off as cool and smart because it's real and not forced.

Do use words that accurately represent the attributes and abilities of your company. *Don't* list words that make you look good on paper, but are unrealistic. *Don't* write words just for the sake of writing them or in the hopes that they will elevate your company or hide some facet of your company. For example, if I owned a "spit and sawdust" hole-in-the-wall pub on the wrong side of the tracks, I would not write *prestigious* as one of my words. I wouldn't be able to deliver on that word, would I?

Or, suppose I ran a cell phone company that routinely charged high fees for "extras" and turned off service for "exceeding account threshold" the day before the bill was sent out when customers were *supposed* to be on a fixed plan that was *supposed* to be the same price every month, *and* the only reason the account thresholds were exceeded was because I *conveniently overcharged* and then made it impossible for my customers to get through to a live person when they called for assistance, *and then*, when my customers finally got through, I gave them attitude as if they were some sort of cell phone criminals when in fact they are probably quite charming and always pay their bills on time . . . if I did that, I really couldn't use the word *friendly*, could I?

Ultimately, you are looking for words that represent truth, the essence of the personality of your business, product, or service. If you want your business to be *prestigious* or *friendly* and it's really not, put that word on another type of list—a list of goals—but leave it off your three-word list. You must always be able to back up your business so that you can stand by your brand.

Guideline 2: Range

Do jot down a wide range of words with different meanings. *Don't* fill your list with synonyms. You can delve into this guideline further as you refine your list, but keep an eye on the range of meanings you are including on your list as you brainstorm. In the end, you want each of your three words to represent a unique dimension of your business identity, not say exactly the same thing with different words.

For example, if one of your final three words is *fun*, then the other two most likely will *not* include *jovial, jolly,* or *entertaining.* Even though each of those words is effective, they have a similar meaning. If the goal is to convey that your business is fun, then only *one* of those words is needed.

Your company represents various personality characteristics, so brainstorm a list that represents a *full range* of them. By all means include all of the authentic words you come up with on what I call your "active list." Just don't expect more than one word with a similar meaning to make the final cut.

Guideline 3: Positioning

Do brainstorm words that fit with your superniche. *Don't* choose words that your superniche would not relate to or, worse, words that might actually alienate that group. Again, you can revisit this guideline in more detail later as you refine your three words, but for now, do consider your positioning—the segment of the population that you aim to attract as your client base—when brainstorming words.

In considering positioning, use the description of your superniche, but also return to some of the questions and answers from the process used to help you define your superniche. The questions will help you come up with more words that may be *different* from those that might otherwise occur to you. For example, who are your favorite customers? Which customers spend the most? What is the average level of education your customers have attained? What is their average income? What are their primary frustrations? What are their commonly held aspirations? What do they value above all else?

Remember that in the first guideline, I stressed the importance of staying true to your brand. In this guideline, I'm asking you to stay true to your superniche. What words would authentically represent *those people*? So if your superniche values economy, you might avoid words like *regal* or *luxurious*. Or, if your superniche aspires to be adventurous, words like *conservative* or *safe* would not accurately represent it.

Remember that these guidelines are just that: guidelines. It is always best to trust your instincts over any guidelines—even over those that *I* offer! If you want a word on your list, write it down. Likewise, if you're not sure whether a word is "good enough," but you like something about it, *write it down.* It may not be worthy of becoming one of your three essential, powerful, earth-shattering words, but then again, it could. Or, it might lead to the perfect word.

CHAPTER 13

Active List

This entire chapter is a series of exercises to help you create an active list of words, from among which you will find three essential, powerful, earth-shattering words that represent your brand. Aim for at least 40 words, but no more than 120. Working in a group is helpful, even if that group is made up of confidants rather than colleagues, because it multiplies the energy and because you can play off one another. Working solo is fine too, of course.

Exercise 1: Generate Words for Three Dimensions: Personality, Attitude, and Values

Get out your timer and set it for 10 minutes, no more and no less. If you are working in a group, do this exercise in silence to avoid passing judgment on one set of words. Once you're done, you can discuss the words and choose those that you like best for your active word list.

Once you start the exercise, keep writing until the timer runs out. It's a bit like automatic writing, and the benefit is that you get really great words that might not have occurred to you if you had stopped to think about what would work best. Remember, there are no wrong words at this stage of the process. Any one of the words could make it to the top three, so write away.

What you're going for here are words that describe the experience of doing business with your company, the three dimensions of your brand identity: personality, attitude, and values. List words that portray the mood, the vibe, the energy, and the spirit of doing business with you.

What words would describe a customer's first impression of your business? What words describe the feeling a frequent customer has when she walks into your establishment? Why do you think people like doing business with you? Besides a product or service, what do your customers get out of doing business with you? What words of praise do you commonly hear from your customers?

Complete the following phrases:

- People do business with my company because we are . . .
- People do business with my company because we provide . . .
- People do business with my company because we aim to . . .
- People do business with my company because they feel . . .
- People do business with my company because they get . . .
- People do business with my company because they experience . . .
- People do business with my company because they like . . .

Look for words that express the attitude and personality of your brand. How do your staff members interact with each other? How would you describe the atmosphere in your office? How do people feel when they visit your place of business? How do you handle phone conversations with customers? How accessible are you to your customers? What aspects of your own personality carry over into your business?

When the 10 minutes are up, move right on to Exercise 2 to keep the momentum going and the creative juices flowing.

Exercise 2: Cultivate Words for Three Dimensions: Personality, Attitude, and Values

Again, set the timer for 10 minutes and get ready to list more words. This time, however, you are going to dig a little deeper. Look past the first impressions and ask detailed, even tough questions to get at the essence of your brand. Remember to shut off your internal censor; if you are brainstorming in a group, set aside judgment and recrimination.

What lurks beneath the surface of your business? What do you wish your customers *really* knew about your business? What would your customers be surprised to learn about your business?

How do you celebrate success? How do you deal with failure? What words describe your rules? What is your attitude toward change? What words describe how you handle adversity, issues, or problems? What is your typical response to good news?

How do you view your competitors? How do they view you? What words describe the way you deal with lackluster employees? How about suppliers who let you down? How do you deal with customers who pay late or not at all? How do you validate good performance? How do you reward top customers? What words come to mind with regard to your company's general attitude toward customers and customer service? How about your company's attitude toward productivity?

What lies beneath your company's attitude toward business in general? What are the underlying themes within your company? How does your company perceive its successes and losses?

Do you see a few negative words on your list? This exercise usually drums up some pretty interesting stuff. Don't fixate on them; even the negative words can lead to something wonderful. Next, you're going to refine the list and find the best words. So reset the timer and let's go!

Exercise 3: Refine Words for Three Dimensions: Personality, Attitude, and Values

By now, you have more than a few words that you are pleased with. This time, setting the timer for another 10 minutes, consider what might be missing from the list. This part is extra fun because you get to fantasize—while still remaining authentic. This means that you're looking for words that reflect your aspirations for your company, but that are also based in reality.

What words can you list that boldly represent the kind of words you have been listing so far? Write down words that take the meanings to the extreme. Think of words you would really like your business to feel like if there were no limits, no horizons.

In this exercise, it may be helpful to think back to when you started your business or your line of work. What inspired you to begin this journey? How did you envision your business or career? What were the goals you aspired to? Try to use descriptive words rather than measurable goals.

In your wildest dreams, what had you hoped to achieve in business? What do you still hope for? Now that you have some experience in business, what are the *new* dreams you have for your brand? List the feelings you would experience if you achieved these dreams and goals.

Write down words that you wish you could have as your own and still be authentic. Remember, this is still just the listing phase; you don't have to commit to any of these words. Just have fun, be creative, and, above all, be daring. This exercise is designed to reveal other character traits that you knew were there, but just had not put your finger on up until now. It is an opportunity to try on words that could be a call to action for you, the next obvious step in your evolution as a business and a brand.

Break Time

By now you should have several pages of words. Feel free to play around with them. Review the answers you gave in the warm-up questions from Chapter 16 and add them to your list. Remember, the most important goal here is to explore and list a range of words that reflect the different aspects of your company and how it is experienced by you, your staff, your vendors, and, most importantly, your marketplace.

Active List

If you got stuck somewhere in the process and came up with only a few words, or if you came up with many words with similar meanings, brainstorm with a friend or colleague or just set your list aside for a day or two. Words will come to you from time to time, and within days you will have at least 40 words to work with.

CHAPTER 14

Organize, Rank, and Review

In the last chapter, you created an active list of dozens of words, among which you will find the three-word persona of your brand. Recall that from your three essential, powerful, earth-shattering words, you can build your entire brand identity with minimum effort and 100 percent authenticity. Everything is easier and more effective when you take the time to discover the three words that best describe the personality, attitude, intent, and experience of your brand.

By the end of this chapter, you will have those three precious words.

Are you excited? Are you having fun? I hope so. It's important for you to enjoy this process, because your attitude right now will inform the process and influence the result.

Remember, this part of your journey is about building the foundation of your brand, which is the personality of your business. The foundation is the bedrock upon which everything else is built, so the last thing you need to do here is rush through the exercises. I am asking you to acknowledge that this is the foundation-building phase of branding, and that in order for you to feel confident in the future, your intentions and focus must be well considered now.

Recall that the Sex Pistols attracted Johnny Rotten and defined not only the band but also the entire punk rock movement with its three words. This is powerful stuff. The image of the experience of doing business with you that people will latch onto in their hearts and minds hinges on these three words. The impression that potential customers will get from your marketing efforts is dependent on these three words. Your three words are the solid ground upon which you will build your World Famous brand.

So as you move forward in the process and begin to narrow down your active word list, I am hoping that you will come from a relaxed place, confident in the knowledge that you are on the exact right path toward building your authentic brand identity.

Before you begin, you'll need to gather a few tools. In addition to your list of words, you will need a dictionary, a thesaurus, and an Internet connection for research purposes. Ready?

Exercise 1: Organize Words for Three Dimensions: Personality, Attitude, and Values

In this exercise, the goal is to organize your active words into three different lists. Use one part logic and two parts instinct. Each list will ultimately be culled down to one word, so the idea here is to group like words together. This does not necessarily mean placing words with similar meanings on the same list. Some words just belong together, as if they evoke a similar feeling or call to action. And yes, some words actually do mean the same thing, and you may feel that it is appropriate to place them in the same group. Again, this is about what *you* think is best, so choose accordingly.

Think of this as being like choosing teams. Start with one player (word) for each team that don't seem to belong together, and then choose players (words) for each team based on how they relate to the first one chosen. Again, steer clear of that dictionary and thesaurus for now, and just generally sort your words into three distinct areas.

If you prefer, think of this exercise in terms of family and extended family. Some words just seem to belong to the same family, and so should be grouped together. As you are grouping words, you will start to see loose patterns. For example, a doctor client of mine was able to group the word *healing* with *progress* and *results.* Another client, a bookkeeper, grouped together *organized, accurate,* and *meticulous* as she went through the process. One of my clients owned a Coyote Ugly–style bar and decided to group words like *freedom* with words like *uncomplicated* and *escape.*

You might also consider organizing your words into three separate dimensions from the perspective of what your business offers. This is not an exact science, and you may find that certain words seem like they could fit on more than one of your lists. Move them around. Consider each word and the feeling it evokes. Play with each list and think about why you chose each word. Continue sorting your active words until you are generally satisfied with each list.

Again, nothing is set in stone yet. As you move on to the next exercises of ranking and filtering your words, you can always go back and reorganize your lists. Also, please don't try to make the lists even. The sorting is important; the number of words on each list is not.

Finally, realize that there are no "wrong" answers. You cannot fail at this task. I have foolproofed this exercise by including several tests at the end of the three-word building process that will help you determine if your three words are a good fit. So relax. Breathe. Have fun. Even if you can't see the finish line, trust that you are on the right path.

Exercise 2: Rank Words for Three Dimensions: Personality, Attitude, and Values

Now you get to pick your favorites, or rather, the words that best fit your business personality. In this exercise, you will rank all the words on your lists using a scale of one to ten, with ten being the best word ever. So, if you really love a word, you might give it a ten, whereas if you think it *could* fit the personality of your business, a five or six would work. If any of the words don't resonate with you at all, give them the lowest score possible.

Ranking anything—be it cars, movies, or even words—requires that you have specific filters. Just as wine connoisseurs judge wines against specific characteristics, such as the nose and the taste, you can use filters to rank your words. Here are the filters I recommend that you use to determine how to rank each word:

Mediocrity

Why bother? When you choose words that everyone else in your industry uses, you risk seeming mediocre. Using words that your competitors may also use makes it nearly impossible to differentiate your brand, and you already know why differentiation is paramount.

Consider the words that your competitors are using or are most likely to choose. Also consider the words that your industry would choose. The idea here is to give low rankings to those words that are commonly used by other businesses in your industry, both direct competitors and related businesses. When you come across a word that would be unique to your company, give it a higher ranking. You get the idea. Your brand can't stand out as the only choice if you cannot distinguish your business personality as being different from *all of the rest.*

This filter will help free you from the doldrums of sameness. Just don't let it steer you away from who you are. You're not going for the opposites here; you're going for authenticity, and you're giving low rankings to words that may be authentic to your business, but are overused in your industry.

For example, if an investment banking company brainstormed the word *conservative*, it might determine that many businesses in its industry already use that word. The investment banking company then gives the word *conservative* a low ranking, but does *not* replace it with a word that means the opposite. The point here is that the word *conservative* is a given in the marketplace; it's overused. Therefore, it's not a good word to use in marketing your own *unique* business personality. So, use this filter to rank the words you already have on your list, not to find new words that have opposite meanings.

Excitement

This filter is easy to employ because it's just acknowledging which words you find most exciting. You get excited when something "just feels right" because you know you're on to something. If a word feels like a good fit for your business, that's reason to be excited. As you go through your lists, rank the words that excite you with high scores. This filter is all instinct, and it very often produces the best results.

Remember, words with negative connotations may actually be the exact words to describe your brand personality. Don't be afraid to give a negative word a high score. Going back to the Sex Pistols example, one of the most exciting words in the band's three-word persona was *obnoxious*, which is normally construed as a negative word. However, it fit the band's brand perfectly, and also served as a call to action.

At one of my seminars, an attorney excitedly chose the word *abrupt*, which most of us would consider a negative trait. Still, it authentically represented his business personality and could be seen as a positive in his industry. In the same audience, a stenographer became excited about *anal-retentive*. Would you want to be called anal-retentive? I'm guessing you'd be quite offended if someone called you that. Yet *anal-retentive* not only accurately described this stenographer but would be seen as an asset in her field.

On a personal note, I actually chose my bookkeeper because when she was a client, a word that excited her was *meticulous*. Do I want a meticulous spouse or best friend? Maybe not. But do I want a meticulous person to take care of my finances and record keeping? Absolutely. In the right context, seemingly negative words very often have positive connotations. And if they are authentic to your business personality, and you are excited by them, by all means give them top rank.

A Call to Action

As you rank the words on your list, consider which words represent a call to action. If a word could effectively spur you on toward greater achievement, it is worthy of a higher ranking. Likewise, if a word could inspire your business to become more unique and distinctive in all areas, rank that word higher than others. Your words are not just representative of your business personality and attitude; they are also an inspiring call to raise the bar. If a word does not fit this criterion, if it does not inspire or motivate you in any way, give it a lower ranking.

At first you may think that all your words make you feel that way. But go through them again one by one and ask yourself if each word really represents a call to action for you or for your company. Does it make you want to change something, or to up the ante on what you're already doing? Does it make you want to be *more* than you already are, or to shift your focus in any way? If not, it's probably more of a static word than a call to action.

The client with the Coyote Ugly–style bar I mentioned earlier chose the word *sassy*. Not only was this word a great fit for the bar's business personality, but it was a call to action in that it directed how the client would approach drawing up new menus, creating new cocktails, and decorating the bar. Likewise, a chiropractor client of mine used the word *empowering* as a call to action that represented his commitment to overall wellness. He answered the call by expanding his focus so that chiropractic care was only part of a bigger program of helping patients achieve wellness.

Exercise 3: Review Words for Three Dimensions: Personality, Attitude, and Values

The hard part is over. Now, go get those three essential, powerful, earth-shattering words and change your business forever.

1. Discard all the low-scoring words on your lists. At least 70 percent of your words should be in the toss pile.

2. Now get out the dictionary and thesaurus. Looking at each of your three lists separately, choose the word that best fits that group. Which word exemplifies the dimension of that group? Which word is the most accurate representation of your business? Which words do you like best? When you select the word, discard the others and move on to the next list.

3. By now you should have three working words. I use the term *working* because you don't have to commit to anything at this point. You are simply trying out three words to see how they feel and fit.

Are you jumping up and down? In my experience, this is the point in the brand-building process when my clients jump up and down because they are either thrilled or frustrated. Yes, frustrated. Even after all of your careful hard work brainstorming, organizing, sorting, and ranking, sometimes the three words you end up with just don't seem to work well together. Something is missing; something isn't quite right. You like two of the words, but the third is not working. Or you like all your words, but you're second-guessing yourself and are worried that there are three better words out there.

If this is how you feel, don't worry. You are on to something, and you will find the right word. Take a break. Sleep on it, even. Then come back to your three words and check the thesaurus to see if there is simply a better word with the same meaning.

Remember, you are still not married to *any* of your words, so if you feel you are almost there, let's just run with your three working words and see how they play out. Think of it as a 30-day money-back guarantee. No commitment. No pressure. If your three words don't feel right or don't fit, you can always return one or all of them for new words, no questions asked.

Ready? In the next chapter, you will take your three working words out for a test drive to see if they are essential, powerful, and, of course, earth-shattering. Ready?

CHAPTER 15

The Test Drive

You know what I love about test-driving new cars? I get to imagine that I am the owner of that car and really get into how it would feel to drive the car every day, how others would view me when I'm driving the car, and if the car feels like "me." For 20 minutes I'm the Jaguar version of me, or the Aston Martin version of me. Will the car meet my expectations? Will it live up to the fantasy?

Twelve years ago, I took the ultimate test drive. One day I gave in to my yearning—yes, yearning—for an Aston Martin and went to look at these cars in a nearby showroom. I hemmed, hawed, and drooled, and then left. I knew I wanted one, I was really excited about getting one, but the price scared me off.

A few weeks later, I received an invitation for me and three friends to test-drive Aston Martins in Napa Valley. Even though I had already decided not to get an Aston Martin, the event sounded like fun, so I set off with three friends for wine country. When we arrived at our destination, we were surprised to discover that there were only six other guests at the event. We had assumed that we would be one of a large group, and that we would get only about two minutes to test-drive the cars. Instead, we were treated to a gourmet lunch—and a key.

There were five cars to choose from, so we split up into pairs and got ready for our adventure. The lead driver told us not to be afraid of pushing the cars. "Go nuts, race each other, really test these puppies out," he said. How cool, I thought, but I really thought he was just saying it for effect. We were about to drive brand-new Aston Martins—I wasn't going to push *anything*.

I put the roof down and followed the lead car. We were enjoying our drive along country lanes when the lead driver drove up beside me, rolled his window down, and said, "Stop being such a wimp. Go for it!"

Wow, he really meant it. I floored it and passed my friends, and soon we were racing each other. Another friend egged me on from the passenger seat, caught up in the moment. We hit the corners at lightning speed, and the car stuck to the road like glue. It was the most exhilarating 45 minutes I've ever experienced. We drove the hell out of those cars. When I started out on the test drive, I had announced that I was not buying an Aston Martin. By the time I got out of that car, I was sold.

Have you ever liked something when you bought it and then returned it because it didn't work out? Sometimes you think you know what you want, and then when you try it out, you realize that it just isn't right. A hotel you loved when you booked it online turns out to be too big and flashy. The couch you liked in the store looks out of place when you bring it home.

The same is true for your three words, and for branding in general. You like the way someone else does things, so you adopt her branding methods as your own. Or, you listen to branding experts and ad agencies because they "know what they're doing." And sometimes you build a brand identity based on your insecurities and fears, choosing something that you *think* will elevate or legitimatize your brand, but that ends up doing the exact opposite. These approaches lack honesty and authenticity, and so how can they ever create a brand that fits?

This is why you need a test drive.

Before you commit to anything, you need to make sure it's a good fit. This is a crucial step in building a World Famous brand identity. So, get a piece of paper, a pen, and a timer. You're going to take those three working words for a spin.

Exercise: Three-Word Test Drive

This exercise has two parts. First, you're going to consider your customers' feelings, and then you're going to describe your three working words in detail. The first part is designed to make sure that your working words will resonate with your superniche, and the second part is designed to make sure that your working words resonate with *you.*

Part 1

What do you already know about your market? Describe how you want your market to feel when doing business with you. At Propaganda, we delivered visual branding packages to top fashion companies. Not only did our clients need to know that the product was going to be exactly right, but they also needed to know that it would arrive dead on time, as the people who would install the packages were flown in specifically for the job. If our shipments were late, our clients would have to send the installation experts home and bring them back again when the packages arrived, losing thousands of dollars.

Our business needed to evoke—and satisfy—a feeling of certainty. Our clients needed to be absolutely certain that the visual branding packages would arrive when promised, without fail. In order to both attract and keep clients, Propaganda had to give our clients a feeling of certainty. So *certainty* became our first word of the three, followed by *fun* and *respect.* (And, as you now know, the word *certainty* has stayed with me through several brands I have created.)

Once you have listed the key feelings you aim to satisfy for your clients, consult your working words to determine how well they would satisfy the feelings you consider important. Do they get the job done? If your working words accomplish your goal, move on to Part 2 of the test drive. If not, revisit the top contenders that you previously discarded and find words that will accomplish this goal.

When I developed this system for branding my own company,

I took my first round of working words for a test drive. Very soon I realized that the words I had chosen for Propaganda did not evoke the feelings I aimed to satisfy in my clients.

Before I went back to the drawing board, I glanced at the list of feelings that I generated in the 10-minute test-drive exercise. There it was—the word I needed. It was on my list of feelings that I found *certainty*, which became one of our three words. All that work, and I found it in the test drive! No matter. It was all worth it, because in the end, I found the three essential, powerful, earth-shattering words that helped build my very own World Famous brand.

Once we had our three words, we used them as an acid test for every idea, every decision, and every plan we made for Propaganda. The word *certainty* showed up in the standards and systems we created. For example, we determined that if a client called to check on an order, then we had failed because we had made the client feel uncertain. We launched a new system that incorporated sending updated progress reports to clients so that they never had to call us to find out about the status of their order. They knew that if we were going to be late, they would be the second to know. We received loads of thanks from clients for the level of certainty we provided and garnered dedicated clients who were thrilled to be doing business with us.

As for *fun*, fun was our middle name. With certainty fully realized in our business, we were able to have plenty of fun. We offered clients a fun experience by creating witty newsletters and funny voicemails, packaging, and billing systems. The word *respect* was an important balancing value. We believed in showing respect across the board, from the receptionist to the president, from our most important customer to the vagrant down the street asking for a quarter. For example, in our warehouse, our guys always helped the UPS driver load orders onto the truck, even though the service contract stated that UPS would do all loading. That kind of respect was repaid many times over. If we ever needed a favor, people showed up. The number of times our skin was saved because a UPS driver decided to come back to pick up excess orders that would not fit onto the truck or made sure that he serviced our business when bad weather or holiday traffic was causing delays for most other people are too many to count.

Our words didn't just show up in package design and brochures; we lived and breathed the personality, attitude, and values of our brand all the way through our company. And you will too, when you have a simple, well-constructed, meaningful, and authentic brand identity. And you are well on your way.

Part 2

Now test all three working words individually in this step. Setting the timer for five minutes, choose one of your three words and, on a fresh piece of paper, write half a page describing what the word means to you. What does the word represent to you? How does it fit your company? What other words does this word incorporate? How do you see yourself putting this word to work in your business? How will it affect your business activity? How might it affect the decisions you make?

This description is about *your* definition of the word, not one from the dictionary. Write as much as you can about the word within the five-minute time frame and stop as soon as the time is up. Repeat the exercise for each of the remaining two words.

How will you know if your test drive worked? Well, it's actually pretty obvious once you start writing. If it's easy for you to complete the exercise in five minutes, the word is working for you. If you feel good about what you're writing, if it starts to make you feel excited, the word is probably a good fit for your business. If describing the word is comfortable for you, as if you could do it in your sleep, you've found a word you can work with.

On the other hand, if you're struggling to finish the exercise, there's a good chance that the word *may* not be the best one for you. If you can't fill up half a page, if the exercise makes you nervous or uncomfortable, or if you simply draw a blank, this "working" word may not work after all. If you find that a word is not passing this part of the test drive, then go back to your high-ranking words, choose another, and repeat this exercise with your new word.

I would caution you to think twice before discarding the word, however. Instead, consider the possibility that you are simply having commitment issues about the word. It could be that you are second-guessing yourself again, afraid to abandon any word in case it may be "the one." Or it could be that a fear of success is taking the pleasure out of your test drive. You're so close to finding your three words that the nervousness you are feeling may have something to do with your fear of taking action using those words.

Remember, it's perfectly okay to come back to this exercise and refine or modify it later on. As you continue to build your World Famous brand identity, you will find yourself reviewing your three words and trying out other words. This reevaluation is healthy and completely worthwhile, as long as it does not hold you back from taking concrete action. In my experience, 50 percent of the people who go through this exercise continue to make changes and fine-tune their word choices even after the test drive.

If all three of your words passed the second part of the test drive, if you feel that your three words are an authentic reflection of the personality of your business *and*, knowing that you don't have to commit to them right now, you feel good about moving forward with them, then let me be the first to congratulate you!

So, what are your three words?

Now that you have them, enter them into your brand profile. (Download your free brand profile document at www.WorldFamous Company.com, press the Brand Profile tab, and enter code WF001.

CHAPTER 16

The Playground of Your Brand

"The brand is an amusement park, and the product is the souvenir."

—NICK GRAHAM, FOUNDER AND CUO (CHIEF UNDERPANTS
OFFICER) OF JOE BOXER

When I was a kid, I loved the Six Million Dollar Man. I pretended to be him all the time, especially in swimming pools. I was living vicariously through the Six Million Dollar Man, playing in the world that he represented. Who did you pretend to be when you were a kid? Wonder Woman? GI Joe? James Dean? Billie Jean King? We live vicariously through others, and through brands. Just look at *InStyle*, a magazine devoted to showcasing the brands that celebrities buy, so that readers can live vicariously through their favorite celebrity by buying the same sheets, jeans, car, or jewelry.

I tell my story of going from blowing my last $20 on booze and fun to being World Famous in seven years whenever I conduct a seminar. Invariably someone will come up to me after the presentation and say, "When I heard you tell that story, I knew you were the guy I wanted to work with." When people relate to your story, they connect to your brand. People want to know the story of your brand: how it started, the funny mishaps and happy accidents, and the heart—above all, the heart. You don't have to educate your customers about your brand; you just have to know it and let them live vicariously through it. Your story is the playground of your brand, and it is what makes your brand identity relatable to your superniche.

This is the vicarious world that the people in your marketplace enter when they use, purchase, or even think about your brand. Beyond your product or service, the playground of your brand is the place you want the people in your marketplace to hang out as soon as your business comes to mind.

The playground does not have to be a real place; rather, it is a place that people can imagine and experience in their mind. Think of your brand as a virtual reality device that, when experienced, transports your customers to a different world. The experience could be as simple as seeing a representation of your brand, or as direct as using your product or service.

Why is your brand playground so important? Because when you live vicariously through something, you never forget it. It makes a permanent imprint on your brain, so that any mention of it elicits the same response.

For example, the playground for my World Famous Company brand identity is "being authentic *and* World Famous." So, when people think of my brand, they are transported to a vicarious world in which they are inspired, and believe that their business can be World Famous too. They remember experiencing a keynote speech, and whenever they think of my brand, they feel the same excitement and energy that they felt the first time they did business with me.

When you live vicariously through something, it becomes part of you. More than that, it becomes *real* for you. When your brand playground appeals to the psychographics of your superniche, it creates a memorable, powerful experience that your clients and customers will want to repeat again and again. Your superniche will be compelled to do business with you because it *gets to live vicariously through your brand.*

One of the ways I differentiate my brand is by adding value to the education I provide, and that value is entertainment—hence info-tainment.

Recall that psychographics are the desires, aspirations, frustrations, and values of a marketplace. On a basic level, the product or service you offer must tap into the psychographic of your superniche (the demographic plus psychographic of your marketplace). The personality of your brand, driven by your three-word persona, must also feed into the psychographic of your superniche. But it is only when you consider the playground of your brand and how it correlates with the psychographic of your superniche that you can truly make an imprint on the hearts and minds of your marketplace.

In terms of adding value for your customers or clients, what could be more powerful than transporting them to a place that fulfills their desires, assuages their frustrations, or calms their nerves? Your brand has the ability to excite your superniche, to satisfy its aspirations and speak to its highest sense of self. Carefully constructed, the playground of your brand can create a fan following like nothing else.

When the playground of your brand is compelling, the people in your superniche will choose to do business with you in order to repeat the experience as often as possible. They will want to "own" a piece of that playground, so that they can access it whenever they want to. An exciting brand playground that speaks to the psychographic of your superniche is the ultimate added value because it is entirely unique to your brand identity and is as potent as the real thing.

The Nick Graham quote at the start of this chapter is one of my favorites because it sums up my concept of the brand playground perfectly. Nick Graham started out selling novelty ties, switched to selling novelty boxer shorts (hence the company name), and built an entire lifestyle brand based on the playground of wacky, outrageous fun. Graham's World Famous company, Joe Boxer, has a carefully constructed vicarious world. Fans of the Joe Boxer brand get to feel silly, funny, and offbeat. The playground is a carefree place, free of rules, obligations, and boring workplace uniforms.

In the Joe Boxer world, customers get to joke around, laugh, and set their worries aside. They get to be kids again. It's a brilliant playground for a company that primarily sells underwear because this is one article of clothing that most people don't see, and so customers get to experience the vicarious world without the risk of appearing inappropriate to the outside world.

Another excellent example of a powerful brand playground is Polo Ralph Lauren, who incidentally also started his company selling neckties. Neckties of a different sort, of course, but like Graham, Ralph Lauren built his brand by consciously thinking about the vicarious world that his customers wanted to live in. Before Ralph Lauren sold his first necktie, he knew he was in the lifestyle business, and that lifestyle was very specific and sophisticated.

From the beginning, Ralph Lauren cultivated a lifestyle playground that allowed his customers to vicariously access a very privileged world. Owning something with the Polo Ralph Lauren brand name is like a having a V.I.P. pass to a lifestyle of refinement, culture, and class. People *feel* as though they are part of that world, and if that playground feeds into their psychographics, they will seek to duplicate that experience again and again.

Ralph Lauren is the godfather of visual branding by way of being the godfather of lifestyle branding. He started using antiques and vintage props in his stores to convey a rich lifestyle that was available only to the elite and wealthy. Ralph Lauren used fine antique furniture, silver trophy cups, classic period luggage and steamer trunks, elegant model sailboats, and sporting photographs depicting men and women from an elegant, bygone era. He knew how to depict the lifestyle that he and his market aspired to live.

The lifestyle that his brand represents stimulates his customers' psychographics in a meaningful way that compels his market to do business with him. He has been heralded as a master of marketing and branding, and many companies, such as Diesel, Tommy Hilfiger, and Banana Republic, have emulated Ralph Lauren's unparalleled success.

Lifestyle branding is especially effective in the fashion industry because what you wear is a personal statement about who you are. But it can be effective in other industries as well, as long as the product or service can also reflect some aspect of your customers' personality and status in life in a public way.

What does the car you drive say about you? What about your laptop or PDA? What about the summer vacation rental you choose each year? Do you see how these items allow you to live in a specific playground in your mind? Do you also see how owning or using these items allows you to become part of a specific lifestyle? Even the magazines or newspapers you read say something about you, your attitude, and your values.

The brand becomes a coveted invitation to an exclusive party, which in most cases is a virtual experience. Some brands take this aspect of adding value even further and actually create a space where their customers can bond and revel in brand ownership. On-line forums for customer chats can be found at countless company web sites. Fan appreciation parties for celebrity, television, and film brands are commonplace in the entertainment industry. Even car companies get in on the action. Remember Saturn's launch campaign? Every owner of a new Saturn received balloons and a party-like presentation when she received her new car, and Saturn held a "family reunion" for car owners that its devoted customers drove thousands of miles to attend.

For Virgin Atlantic, the playground is quite literal. You already know that Virgin Atlantic is actually in the entertainment industry, not the airline industry. Building on that, you can see that Richard Branson constructed a very specific brand playground when he started Virgin Atlantic: a place where his customers could party and indulge, all the while defying the status quo. He goes to great lengths to create an *actual* world that represents his maverick personality and rebellious nature.

Yet Virgin also has a vicarious playground, which is the feeling that is elicited in people at the mere mention of the brand. I know that whenever *I* think about doing business with Virgin Atlantic or Virgin America, I am elated because I am *reliving* the experience of every flight I have ever taken with them. I want to recreate that experience, so I rearrange my schedule in order to accommodate whichever Virgin flight is available.

Some entrepreneurs, such as Nick Graham, Ralph Lauren, and Richard Branson, realize the playground of their brand immediately. Others (like me, for instance) take a journey to get there. You've heard a lot about how I transformed my failed antique business into a multimillion-dollar visual branding business, and how our biggest client, Polo Ralph Lauren, served as a catalyst in that story. But it was in discovering the playground of my company's brand that we were able to get Polo as a client in the first place.

Remember my story about when my business partner and I attended our very first Visual Merchandising and Store Design show and successfully channeled our efforts into the visual merchandising industry? Despite our best efforts and other big-name clients, there was one account I could never seem to get near, the elusive mother of all visual merchandising accounts: Polo Ralph Lauren. I wanted this account with a passion because, after all, Ralph Lauren had created the niche that enabled companies like mine to exist. Yet no matter what I did, Polo Ralph Lauren just didn't respond to my efforts.

One day I enthusiastically attended a seminar given by the great motivational speaker Anthony Robbins. Transfixed, I began to see that I was playing small. I realized that there were many more ways to approach business, and that I had to focus on the *needs* of my marketplace rather than the products I was selling.

The concepts I learned that day stayed with me and occupied my mind for weeks. I subjected myself to relentless questions. Driving down the freeway, in the shower, from the moment I woke in the morning until I closed my eyes to sleep, I would ask myself the same series of questions: What do my clients need? What do my clients *really* need?

I kept on thinking and thinking and thinking, hoping to come up with a clever new display idea or a unique arrangement of antiques. But I knew that I was still thinking too small, too literally. Soon after the Anthony Robbins seminar, I was talking with Paul, a client who was in charge of purchasing for Dillard's department store chain out of Little Rock, Arkansas. He was going on and on about how Dillard's had a hard time being distinctive, how he sometimes felt that everything was just one big blur of sameness.

"What we need is some sort of differentiation," Paul said.

Differentiation. Differentiation. D-I-F-F-E-R-E-N-T-I-A-T-I-O-N!

Suddenly it dawned on me that while we were in the visual merchandising industry, we actually provided something much more specific than that. We provided differentiation. Oh, my goodness *gracious*! It was nirvana. I had finally connected the dots and discovered what our clients needed and how our business could provide it to them. Store chains weren't investing in antiques or simply buying antiques in order to have them; they were trying to stand out from the crowd. Our clients were trying to make a statement that they were different from one another, just as Ralph Lauren had accomplished in the stores I had admired for so long. How could I have been so stupid as not to realize this before?

But now I did get it. Hallelujah! With this realization, the whole world changed. Within a couple of months, we had shifted our entire sales and marketing approach. We put together prop packages based on themes, so that our clients were able to easily choose how they wanted to be different. Now, rather than choosing individual display items that got lost in the shuffle and appeared to be identical to those used at competing stores, our clients could choose a package that would help them differentiate their store in a cohesive way with maximum impact.

For example, our Gentleman's Packages consisted of English leather suitcases and trunks, trophy cups, framed 1920s photographs, vintage typewriters and globes, wooden radios, and antique mantel clocks. Companies such as Dillard's, Macy's, May Company, Parisian, and Belk, Federated Department Stores bought many of these packages to differentiate their men's clothing departments.

Our Urban Packages included 1950s hubcaps and chrome fenders, an assortment of gas and oil cans, and old gas station advertising boards and signage; they were big hits with companies like Aeropostale and Sears for their work wear departments. And our Nautical Packages featured beautiful model sailboats, pairs of oars, fishing poles, wicker baskets and catcher's nets, glass floats, and even coils of thick, old rope. Such packages went to Nautica and various other specialty retailers.

Once we started presenting our theme packages and promoting ourselves as experts in the field of differentiation, business flourished. We added significant value from doing business with us by carefully cultivating our vicarious playground that was differentiation. It was the place our clients hung out whenever they even thought about doing business with us. We were the company that could provide visual merchandising packages that would enable them to stand out, and the mere mention of our name conjured up the vicarious world of differentiation. This made them feel good about themselves, and good about their decision to do business with us.

We knew that in order to really take our business to the next level, we needed to stay ahead of visual merchandising trends, so that we had truly unique packages to offer our clients. The visual merchandising industry is cyclical, and some stores end up with very similar if not identical display items. So, we became trendsetters, allowing our clients to tap into that world as well.

Eventually, the tide turned away from antiques and vintage themes, but we were ready. And then it happened. Polo Ralph Lauren, the company that had ushered in the era of antique and vintage visual merchandising, was ready to launch a new trend, and it wanted us to help it do so. After all my attempts to get Polo to notice me, here it was knocking on *my* door. The word was out about our company. The buyer at Dillard's advised Polo Ralph Lauren that we were experts in differentiation, and that did the trick.

One week later we signed a 400-store rollout deal at the Polo Ralph Lauren offices in New York City. The company hired us because we had already established ourselves as the "go-to guys" for differentiation long before we even met with company representatives. Our reputation—our brand personality and playground— preceded our meeting with Polo, and our ability to deliver on all that our brand promised closed the deal. For Polo Sport, a luxury sportswear line, we differentiated the brand by focusing on the spirit of Polo: freedom, prestige, and a refined, yet rugged lifestyle.

The Evolution of My Playground

When we operated as London Antique Emporium, we went about our day believing that we were antique dealers. By default, the playground of our brand was "antique business." When I realized that we were actually in the visual merchandising industry, I assumed that our playground was "visual merchandising." But as the previous story illustrates, I soon came to realize that the playground of our brand was "differentiation."

We were still selling the same products—antiques and vintage items—yet we were focused on transporting our marketplace to a world where it could think about standing out from the competition. After years of fine-tuning our brand identity, we realized that our playground was the field of differentiation. But did we stop there? No. We kept refining our superniche and our brand personality, and we kept adding value in myriad ways, including the modification of our brand playground.

Later, after Polo Ralph Lauren asked us to help it redefine Polo Sport, we realized that we were not in the visual merchandising industry; we were in the branding industry. After the near miss with Tommy Hilfiger, we changed our name to Propaganda and began referring to our company as "visual branding specialists."

Each step of our journey brought more opportunity—opportunity for clarification, growth, and success. It was a long journey. Propaganda grew to be a multimillion-dollar business, and through that journey I came to my own realizations about my life's passion. I sold my share of Propaganda to my former business partner and set off to chart a new course: to help individuals and businesses develop their own World Famous brands. (Eventually my former business partner closed Propaganda for personal reasons.)

Fortunately, your journey can be significantly shorter. Every step gets you closer to a tightly defined mission; a refined approach to doing business, and a succinct, powerful brand identity that resonates in the hearts and minds of your marketplace.

To create a kick-ass brand identity, you have to get people so excited about your business and the vicarious playground associated with the brand that they just *have to* buy a product (or engage a service) to say that they were there. The people in your superniche must be so thrilled with your brand and all that it represents—tapping into psychographics and building on the three-word persona—that they feel compelled to do business with you, to get a souvenir from the amusement park that is your brand.

Exercise: What Is Your Brand Playground?

This exercise is about finding the playground of your brand identity—what people get from living in your world, if only for a few minutes. Each of the four parts of this exercise is designed to get you to the same destination—the discovery of your brand playground—using different routes.

Please read through all four exercises before you begin, and choose the one that seems to make the most sense to you. If you still haven't arrived at a definite brand playground, move on to the next one until you find one that feels right and fits with your superniche and with the personality, attitude, and values of your brand identity.

The first part of this exercise will help you discover your playground through writing a brief summary of the evolution of that playground. In Part 2 you will seek out your playground through exploring the highest purpose of your business. The third part of this exercise will help you find your playground by way of your industry. The final part of this exercise will get you there in a different way: by posing several questions that, when answered, will lead you to your brand playground.

Part 1

Go back a few pages and reread the evolution of the playground of my former company, Propaganda. In brief, write the history of your brand, citing the industries in which your business has operated and what you think the playground of your brand most likely was. It does not have to be well written, and it should be no more than two paragraphs. Use a bulleted list if you prefer.

Remember, every business has a brand playground, but, just as my first playground was "antique business," it is often chosen by default. What were your default brand playgrounds? What industry do you operate in now, and what is the current playground for your brand?

Looking at the evolution of your brand identity, what thoughts do you have about the future of your brand playground? Are you happy with the playground you currently have, or does it need to be refined or modified in some way?

Part 2

The playground of your brand can be part of the evolution of your company, especially when it is based on the highest purpose of your business. Cultivating your brand playground helps you to both see that purpose and rise to the challenge of *becoming* that purpose. Often, the playground of your brand is synonymous with your highest purpose.

Write down the highest purpose of your business. This is not about financial goals or market share. This is about what drives you (or your business) to keep reaching out, to keep on; very often it is about what prompted you to start your business (or your career) in the first place. It could be about meaning, or innovation, or community. Perhaps it is about connection, transformation, or inspiration. Whatever it is—whatever you have to offer that is deeper than dollars and of a higher purpose than paper success—write it down.

Now, how could your higher purpose become the playground of your brand? Is it possible that it *already is* the playground of your brand? Remember, this does not have to be complex; for Joe Boxer, the playground represents fun and individuality. Perhaps you have a printing company and your higher purpose is to protect the environment by using recycled and environmentally friendly products. This higher purpose could also be the playground of your brand, in that your brand identity would represent an eco-friendly playground where other concerned citizens could feel welcome and at ease.

Part 3

You've already done the important work of defining the industry in which your business truly operates, and you can build on that work in cultivating the playground of your brand. For example, you already know that Polo Ralph Lauren is in the lifestyle business. In tightening that definition further, you arrive at Polo's brand playground, a specific *type of lifestyle* that is prestigious, exclusive, and refined.

In a previous exercise in Step 3, you defined the industry in which your business *truly* operates, which is not necessarily what you do or what you sell. Ideally, that definition is short. Now expand on the length of the description, but tighten the focus.

1. Write down the industry in which your business operates.

2. Industry definitions are generally broad, but playgrounds are very specific. In what unique way does your business operate in this industry? For example, Virgin Atlantic is an airline that is in the entertainment industry, and it provides entertainment in an upscale, hip, super-cool way.

3. How does your business fit the psychographics of your superniche, and what does that tell you about the playground of your brand? For example, the superniche of Polo Ralph Lauren is people from affluent communities who want luxury, value exclusivity, and aspire to be admired and worldly. (See the Brand Profile* exercise from Step 2.) Polo Ralph Lauren's playground is an elite, wealthy, cultured lifestyle, which fits the psychographics of its superniche.

4. What benefits does your business provide to your customers or clients? For example, my former company, Propaganda, realized the playground of our brand in part by identifying a benefit that we provided to our clients. When we discovered that we were able to provide the tools with which our clients could differentiate their brands, our playground became "differentiation." Eventually, when our industry evolved from visual merchandising to branding, the ultimate benefit that we provided our clients was "sophistication."

*Download your free brand profile document at www.WorldFamousCompany.com, press the BRAND PROFILE tab, and enter code WF001.

Part 4

Do you remember how in the previous story I kept asking questions about my business and what my clients needed, and then eventually it hit me? Differentiation was my playground (although I didn't refer to it as a "playground" at the time).

Sometimes brainstorming through asking a series of questions will get you to the same place: a lightbulb, "aha!" moment that is hard to come by when you simply ask, "What is the playground of my brand?" Some of the following questions may seem identical to previously asked questions, but they are actually asked in different ways to shake up your brain and get you thinking in a new direction. Again, try to answer them as quickly as possible, using a timer if it helps you to stay on task.

1. Where do you want your business—what you do or what you sell—to take people?

2. Where do you want your brand to take people?

3. What do you want the people in your superniche to feel when they see, think about, or use your brand?

4. What are you *really* selling?

5. What is it that you *think* you do and what business do you *think* you're in?

6. How do you classify yourself or your company in the business world?

7. What steps do you take so that your business fits into that classification?

8. What compliments do you hear most frequently about your business, your staff, and your product or service?

9. What is the highest and best use of your product or service?

10. How do you want your customers to feel when they think of your company? Be as specific as possible. Simply saying, "I want them to feel great" is not specific enough. How exactly do you want them to "feel great"?

11. What feelings does your product, service, or business as a whole elicit in your client base?

12. In what ways would you like to develop your business, product, or service further?

13. What needs are you truly attempting to satisfy in people?

14. When you visualize doing business with your clients, how exactly do you satisfy them?

15. What are you really, ultimately selling beyond your product or service?

Exercise: Test-Drive Your Playground

Like your three-word persona, your brand playground is a work in progress. The first order of business is to test-drive your ideas, using the same methodology as in previous exercises. In other words, you've already completed one test drive, so this one will be a piece of cake!

If you haven't defined your playground yet, I dare you to go back and complete the previous exercise. Please. Thank you.

Please limit yourself to no more than 10 minutes for each of the following questions.

1. What is the playground of your brand, and what inspired you to choose it?

2. How is your brand playground a call to action for your business and, for extra credit, how is it a call to action for your marketplace?

3. How could you use your brand playground as an acid test for the way you do business and the way you communicate with your marketplace?

4. Assuming that your brand playground excites you (which it should), in what way are you excited by the idea?

How did your brand playground do on the test drive? Did it pass with flying colors?

Exercise: Describe Your Brand Playground

In this step, you will name and describe the playground of your brand. For example, if you were Ralph Lauren, you might include the following in your brand profile:*

Polo Ralph Lauren's Brand Playground

The playground of the Polo Ralph Lauren brand is an elite, wealthy, cultured lifestyle. The playground speaks to the aspirations of the brand's superniche, allowing consumers to experience the world of luxury and refinement even if they are not part of that lifestyle. Consumers access this vicarious world at the mention of the Polo Ralph Lauren brand, and they achieve the ultimate playground experience in purchasing an item with that brand.

And if you were Richard Branson, you might include the following descriptions in your brand profile:*

Virgin Atlantic's Brand Playground

The Virgin Atlantic playground is super-cool, hip, and a bit naughty, speaking to the psychographics of the brand's superniche. In doing business with Virgin Atlantic, consumers are able to experience a literal and vicarious world of luxury and entertainment that is totally unique and addictive.

Just knowing the playground of your brand has a transformative effect on your business and your brand. Knowing it's there, whether you choose it or not, puts you miles ahead of other businesses in your industry. Cultivating it, refining it, and living up to it will take your brand to the next level—the *World Famous* level.

*Download your free brand profile document at www.WorldFamousCompany.com, press the BRAND PROFILE tab, and enter code WF001.

CHAPTER 17

Declaring the Promise of Your Brand

The final step in differentiation, and the final step in building your brand profile, is declaring the promise of your brand. You've worked hard to get to this point, and anticipating the exciting step to come (Ready, Set, Engage!) may tempt you to simply skim this chapter and move on. I urge you to read on with an open and fresh mind, because understanding and implementing the information covered in this chapter could be the difference between a flash-in-the-pan brand and a World Famous brand with legions of die-hard fans.

Every World Famous brand, and I do mean *every World Famous brand,* holds true to a promise that the marketplace can count on. A business that is designed simply to chase the almighty dollar will lose sight of its authenticity and eventually become irrelevant. But when a business makes a promise to its marketplace that can be trusted and believed in, it can inspire masses of people to line up to do business with it.

The promise of your brand could be related to creating positive change by giving back to the world, such as donating a percentage of your profits to charity or funding a philanthropic division of your business. Look at Rosie's Shop, Rosie O'Donnell's online store that donates 100 percent of its profits to her foundation to help underprivileged children. The promise of her brand is that every penny earned on her Rosie-related merchandise will fund various charitable organizations related to the needs of children. So when customers go to purchase T-shirts and other items chosen by Rosie O'Donnell, they know that they are not funding her life of wealth and privilege, they are helping Rosie help kids.

The promise of your brand could also have to do with the aspects of your business where you refuse to compromise, such as the quality of your ingredients or the benefits offered to your employees. A great example of this promise is Mrs. Fields Cookies. From the beginning, Debbi Fields refused to compromise on the quality of her ingredients. When the price of pecans skyrocketed, she was encouraged to purchase pecans of a lower quality in order to keep costs down. But Debbi refused. The promise of Mrs. Fields Cookies was that customers would always get a cookie made from the best ingredients available. (Incidentally, this was part of the reason why Debbi was able to charge a premium price for her cookies.)

Your promise could also be directly related to benefiting your customer base, such as staying open all day every day or accepting all returns without an explanation. Take Perdue, the number one brand of fresh chicken on the East Coast. Perdue's brand promise is that it practices humane treatment of poultry and never gives its chickens antibiotics, hormones, or steroids. While some companies do not promote their brand promise, Perdue makes sure that every commercial states its commitment to providing natural, fresh chicken. Adhering to strict requirements from monitoring agencies and sharing that information with customers via its web site allows Perdue to prove that it can back up its brand promise.

The promise of your brand may have to do with your company's mission, such as improving labor conditions or inventing products to improve lives. The Body Shop, an eco-friendly cosmetics, body, and hair-care product line, is aligned with its mission to "save the planet." This company believed in this promise decades before it was fashionable, and it has never wavered from its mission, the promise of its brand. Using ingredients that are environmentally friendly and biodegradable and creating products that have not been tested on animals deliver on The Body Shop's promise. For The Body Shop, it was never about creating the best shampoo. It was always about saving the world's resources.

There is an intrinsic, overriding promise behind every brand, and you need to know what that promise is. Your promise is a declaration to the marketplace and to the world at large that allows you to position your business for maximum results. Declaring your brand promise adds meaning and intention to your brand identity and reveals the soul of your business. Your superniche needs to know what you stand for in order to get 100 percent behind your brand.

In declaring the promise of your brand, you create direction and momentum for your business. This declaration is absolutely one of the most important things you can ever, ever do to build a World Famous brand. It takes your company from three-dimensional to out of this world; it is the difference between an ambivalent marketplace and a superniche that can't wait to spread the word about its new find, *your* fantastic business.

Above all, this declaration is a promise that can never be broken. It is a promise that you would not give up for a million dollars. If you would be willing to give up your promise, set it aside temporarily, or even just compromise on it slightly in order to save money, time, or face, then it's not a promise. It's a notion. It may even be a goal. But until you commit to it fully, it is not a promise.

Your brand promise can be a phrase or a sentence. It is usually not just one word, as in the three personality words that make up the foundation of your brand. In fact, the promise of your brand is very often quite different from your three-word persona. It is more likely to stem from your personal beliefs as a business owner or founder, or, if you are on a career path, from the founding mission of the company you work for. But it can also come from a traditional place of adding value, such as a benefit or guarantee that your business stands behind.

In some cases, the promise of the brand is closely related to the playground of the brand, with the vicarious world in which the marketplace hangs out when thinking of a brand being directly related to the promise of that brand. The Body Shop would be an example of this, with customers reveling in the "save the planet" playground provided by this eco-friendly retailer.

This final step in building a World Famous brand piggybacks on the work you did in the previous chapter, the exercises related to the higher purpose of your business. Your brain is already poised and ready to think about the promise of your brand. Once you determine your brand promise, you will be inspired to declare it, own it, and live up to it. It will reignite your passion for your business and your brand, and will fuel your company with heart and soul. Reaching that fourth dimension of your brand identity makes you unstoppable. It makes you World Famous.

Exercise: What Is the Promise of Your Brand?

Your company may already have a brand promise, but may not be aware of it. Or you may know exactly what your brand promise is, but you have not yet declared it to your marketplace. Many of you will not have a specific brand promise, or may not be sure which of the benefits, guarantees, and other ways in which you add value for your clients and customers is the definitive, overriding promise of your brand.

This exercise will help you zero in on the promise of your brand, and then test it out to make sure that it is in line with the brand building you have done so far. Take a little time with this one. Answer the questions with your higher purpose in mind. Worry about your marketplace later. For now, just speak from the heart.

1. In what aspects of your business do you refuse to compromise? Why? What is behind that standard?

2. What are the ethics of your industry, and how do you adhere to them?

3. What benefits, guarantees, and other added value do you provide to your customers or clients? Which of these are unique to your business or your industry?

4. What are your core values? If they are different, what are the core values of your company?

5. What is the mission, the higher purpose of your company?

6. How do you contribute—or hope to contribute—to society?

7. How would you like to make an impact on your neighbor-hood? Your community? Society as a whole?

8. What are the causes that resonate with you and inspire you to help in any way you can?

9. What aspects of your business are you unwilling to change, no matter what the cost to or impact on your business?

10. What standards, ethics, or values do you aspire to embody?

Exercise: Test-Drive Your Brand Promise

The previous exercise was designed to help you discover your brand promise. In this exercise, you will test-drive this promise so that you can declare it with confidence. Sometimes people initially come up with a brand promise that sounds good on paper, but does not accurately reflect their business. Or sometimes the promise of the brand is not congruent with the psychographics of its superniche. Answer the following questions as quickly as possible in order to gain that gut-level response.

1. What is the promise of your brand? What made you single out this aspect of your business as the overriding promise?

2. How is your brand identity a call to action for you, your business, and your marketplace?

3. How does the promise of your brand fit the psychographics of your superniche? How does it appeal to these people's values, aspirations, or frustrations?

4. How does the promise of your brand complement the foundation of your brand, the three-word persona?

5. Does the promise of your brand excite you? Does it excite your staff or your colleagues?

Exercise: Describe Your Brand Promise

In this step, you will name and describe the promise of your brand. For example, if you were Ralph Lauren, you might include the following in your brand profile:*

Polo Ralph Lauren's Brand Promise

The promise of the Polo Ralph Lauren brand is superior quality and exclusivity. The brand consistently delivers the finest-quality merchandise that represents an exclusive lifestyle of refinement and luxury.

Or, if you were Richard Branson, you might include the following in your brand profile:*

Virgin Atlantic's Brand Promise

The promise of the Virgin Atlantic brand is that it will never submit to the status quo. The brand is steadfast in its dedication to a rebellious attitude that is never, ever boring and is always fun and exciting.

---

*Download your free brand profile document at www.WorldFamousCompany.com, press the BRAND PROFILE tab, and enter code WF001.

Differentiation, the Secret Weapon

What makes a customer choose your business over another business? The people in your superniche prefer you because the personality of your brand resonates with them on an emotional level. You are different in a way that is meaningful to them. Your business stands out among the crop of similar businesses because you reflect an identity based in authenticity. You're real. You're different. *You know who you are, and you cause your market to feel good about itself in choosing you.*

Differentiation is key if your brand is to stand out as the only choice in your marketplace. But before you can differentiate your business, you first have to realize which industry your business *truly* operates in. What you do or sell is not necessarily your industry; in fact, very often it is *not* your industry. Your industry is less about your product or service and more about the experience of doing business with your company and the meaning behind your product or service.

For example, you may think that because your business deals in mountain bikes, you are in the bike sales industry when, in fact, you are in the adventure industry. Or depending on your approach to business and the psychographics of your superniche, you could be in the fitness industry, or the competitive sports industry, or the green industry helping to save the planet.

Once you have defined your industry, you can go about discovering and cultivating an authentic business personality and attitude. By default or out of fear, it's common for businesses to adopt a boring personality. Yet just as your personality is an important factor in fostering personal relationships, the personality and attitude of your brand are essential in connecting with your marketplace, your superniche. Put two businesses with equal merits side by side, and the consumer will choose the one with a vital, authentic personality every time. When you blend in, you are boring, and being boring is the kiss of death in any relationship, especially with your marketplace.

To build a strong, World Famous brand, you need to be able to define your personality using three succinct words—three essential, powerful, earth-shattering words. Your three words serve as the foundation of your brand identity, unifying all aspects of your business. Your three words are both an acid test and a call to action, serving to define who you are and then turn up the volume on that persona. The three words are vital because they are used to stimulate the psychographics of your superniche and create raving fans who see you as the definitive business in your marketplace, the only choice.

An often overlooked and immensely powerful way to build a kick-ass brand identity is through the development of the vicarious world that is the playground of your brand. This place, though it is mostly imaginary, is where the people in your marketplace hang out in their minds at the mere mention of your brand. When people live vicariously through something, they never forget it, as is true with the vicarious world your brand provides. Appealing to the psychographics of your superniche, the playground of your brand is an experience that your customers and clients will seek to repeat over and over again.

One of the key ways in which you create a World Famous brand identity is by cultivating excitement about your business through the playground of your brand, so that people in your marketplace must own a piece of that playground just to say they were there. Purchasing your products or engaging your services allows your marketplace to tap into that vicarious playground at will.

The final step in creating your brand identity is to declare a brand promise that your marketplace can believe in. In order to achieve maximum results, the promise of your brand must ring true to the mission, values, and personality of your brand. It must come from the heart.

The promise of your brand could be based on your desire to contribute to the world, or it could have to do with the standards or ethics of your business, or it could complement the mission of your company, or it could be based on creating a benefit or guarantee for your customer base. A simple phrase or sentence, the promise of your brand is one that can never be broken, and so it should be taken on with a steadfast commitment.

Recap of Exercises in Step 3

In this step, you completed a lot of very important brand-building work. The sheer volume of exercises in this step calls for a recap, but if you haven't read the step yet, I encourage you to at least read each exercise in its entirety to get the full benefit. That said, here's what was explored in Step 3:

1. *Define your industry.* What ideas does your company represent, and how do those ideas relate to your industry? What are the ultimate benefits you are providing to your customer?

2. *Boardroom design.* Describe your boardroom or conference room. What does it reveal about your business personality? If you don't have a boardroom, describe the place in which you meet your marketplace, your customers or clients. Then design a boardroom (meeting place) that would reflect the unique personality of your brand.

3. *Three-word warm-up.* Describe in three words your neighbors, your least favorite teacher, the last restaurant you visited, the last web site you visited, the strangest place you've

ever been, and so on. Also, describe yourself in three words. The goal of this exercise is to warm up your brain and train it to think about how to describe something uniquely and specifically using three words.

4. *Brainstorm an active word list.* Considering your brand's authenticity, range, and positioning, brainstorm an active list of 40 to 120 words that describe the personality and attitude of your brand. This process breaks down into three separate exercises: generate, cultivate, and refine.

5. *Organize.* Separate the active word list into three categories or dimensions based on similarities, but not necessarily words with similar dictionary definitions.

6. *Rank.* Give each word a score from one to ten, with ten being the highest, using the filters of mediocrity (similarity to competitors and other businesses in your industry), excitement, and whether or not the word serves as a call to action.

7. *Review.* Cut the low-scoring words and then choose one word from each of the three dimensions. Now you have three working words.

8. *Test drive.* Take your three words for two test drives to see if they are the best, most authentic, most powerful words for your business. First, list the feelings that you would like your brand to evoke in your superniche and then determine if your three words evoke those feelings. Second, write a half-page definition of each of your three words to see how well the word resonates with you and how well you understand it.

9. *Discover your brand playground.* What is the vicarious world that people in your marketplace enter when they come into contact with your brand?

10. *Declare the promise of your brand.* What is your company's higher purpose? What is your higher purpose? What does your brand implicitly and consistently promise to your customers?

Whew! You really worked hard to differentiate your brand identity, and it shows. I'd like to take this moment to congratulate you. Finding your three words is no small feat, and you did a great job. Keep the words handy as you continue with the brand-building process. Remember, nothing is set in stone. You can always go back and tweak them. This is *your* business and *your* World Famous brand. Now, for the final exercises of this step, you're going to add your three words to your brand profile, and then write your brand identity statement.

Exercise: Adding Personality to Your Brand Profile

At the end of Step 2, you started building your brand profile. You wrote a brand overview that encapsulated what you do or sell, listed your primary demographic, and then described the psychographic profile of your superniche.

In this step, you will add the fruits of your hard work in Step 3, your three-word persona. The task is simple: Add your three essential, powerful, earth-shattering words to your brand profile. After each word, write a short descriptive summary of *your* definition of the word. Use the powerhouse brands Polo Ralph Lauren and Virgin America for examples again.

If you were Ralph Lauren, your three words and their definitions might look like this:

> **Prestigious:** *It's about bringing distinguished, upper-class status to all who wear the Polo Ralph Lauren label. It's impressive, strong, and worldly. It's about achieving influence, and it's about the allure of old money. The word* prestigious *might show up at Polo Ralph Lauren in the events the company sponsors and in its affiliations, choosing partners that are known to be exclusive and prestigious.*

> **Refined:** *It's about being the epitome of sophistication, elegance, and superior quality. It's about having a gracious, cultured existence, one that is not based on trend or productivity. It's also about being flawless, uncompromising, and beautiful. The word refined might show up at Polo Ralph Lauren in the design of the retail stores, creating an atmosphere of refinement.*

> **Lifestyle:** *It's about a way of being and a standard of living that sets us apart and elevates us from others. It's about living up to*

an idea of perfection in every aspect of our lives, from clothing to home furnishings. The word lifestyle *might show up at Polo Ralph Lauren in the brand's television commercials and magazine ads showcasing the lifestyle coveted by the ideal Polo customer.*

And if you were Richard Branson, your three words and their definitions might look like this:

Rebellious: *It's about defying industry rules and standards, challenging the status quo, refusing to conform to societal norms and codes of conduct, pushing the envelope, irreverence, doing it my way despite the opposition. The word* rebellious *might show up at Virgin Atlantic in its launch and promotional events, highlighting the rebellious nature of Richard Branson and the company.*

Champion: *It's about being a hero for my cause, which is anticonformity, and for my customers, who want to get behind someone who is willing to challenge the conventional wisdom. It's also about being excellent, possessing a winning spirit, and winding up on top every time. The word* champion *might show up at Virgin Atlantic in its approach to customer service, making passengers feel part of a special group of people.*

Maverick: *It's about venturing out on my own, separate from the group. It's about being unorthodox, independent, and completely free of debts, ties, and obligations to any authority. It's also about being wild, brave, and bold. The word* maverick *might show up at Virgin Atlantic in its upending of the standard rules of airline travel, offering perks and privileges that other airlines do not.*

Now that you see how Ralph Lauren and Richard Branson might summarize their three-word descriptions, add your three words to your brand profile.

Exercise: The Brand Identity Statement

A brand identity statement is packed with motivation, inspiration, and dedication. It speaks to the soul and the higher purpose of your brand. It encapsulates the essence of your brand identity and serves as the ultimate acid test and call to action. It is like your very own Declaration of Independence, your call to action based on passion, answering your higher purpose and breaking free from the status quo.

Your brand identity statement is made up of three parts: the three-word persona, the playground, and the promise. In other words, this exercise should be a walk in the park, seeing as you already have each of the three components of your statement. Still, please don't jump ahead just because you have all three separate elements. This exercise is essential because it creates a cohesive, powerful statement that will embolden you at first sight.

1. Write down your three-word persona, the description of your brand playground, and the promise of your brand.

2. Combine all three components into one succinct statement. For example, Polo Ralph Lauren might have the following brand identity statement:

> *Polo Ralph Lauren is a* prestigious, refined lifestyle *brand that provides access to an* elite world of wealth, culture, and class *with the promise of* superior quality and exclusivity.

In this example, Polo's three words are *prestigious, refined,* and *lifestyle.* The vicarious playground of the Polo Ralph Lauren brand is an "elite world of wealth, culture, and class." Finally, the promise of the brand is "superior quality and exclusivity."

3. Once you have a tight, authentic brand identity statement, try it out for size. Read it over a few times. Read it aloud. Share it with your friends, family, and colleagues. What kind of response do you get from your peers and confidants? How do you feel when you read your statement?

4. If an aspect of your brand identity statement does not sit well with you, it may be time to go back to one of the previous exercises and refine your three-word persona, your playground, or

your brand promise. Trust your instincts. You know who you are and what your brand is all about.

Your brand identity statement should reflect the unique truth and personality of your brand, so keep at it until you are totally thrilled each time you read it. It should give you chills. Goose-bumps. And perhaps a tiny tinge of nervous anticipation. After all, your brand is about to enter the realm of World Famous. That's more than a little reason to feel nervous and excited.

One more step, and your profile will be complete. Then it's time to use it as you work to engage your market. You're so close!

Add Value

It all started when a hairdresser offered a customer a cup of coffee while she was waiting to get her hair cut, and then everyone wanted in. That simple cup of coffee created a feeling of added value, so that the customer viewed the experience of doing business with her hairdresser as being *worth more* than the experience at other hair salons.

Today that same salon may have to be a little more creative in order to stand out among the throngs of hairdressers offering coffee to customers. Perhaps now it's special restorative tea from Indonesia and neck massages with organic oils. Whatever the added value is, it's another reason why consumers choose one business over another.

In a world in which consumers have a seemingly endless array of choices, it's your job to increase the attraction of your company by adding value to your own offering. It's the next step in differentiating your brand identity.

With your superniche clearly defined; the personality, attitude, and values of your brand firmly in place; and the vicarious world and brand promise clearly defined, adding value becomes a piece of cake. You know that the value you add must fit the psychographic of your marketplace *and* your three-word persona, so that your efforts to add value will be successful and make a real impact.

Starbucks is a great example of a business that added value in a powerful, brand-defining way. Walk into any Starbucks and take a look around. Can you spot the added value that helped to put this World Famous brand on the map? I'll give you a clue: When was the last time you felt that you had outstayed your welcome at Starbucks? Unless you tried to camp out there for the night, I'll bet that you have never felt uncomfortable sitting at Starbucks. That's the added value that catapulted this Seattle-based coffee company and its $5 coffee drinks into the consciousness of every person in America.

Starbucks went global some time ago, so you may not remember what it was like when you first walked into one. Part of the appeal of Starbucks was—and is—that you could sit there all day and no one would bother you. Once you take your seat, the Starbucks's staff leaves you completely alone, whether you purchase anything or not.

Conduct meetings and interviews, meet back-to-back blind dates, work on your laptop for eight hours straight, or even host a book club event—Starbucks doesn't mind, and you don't need its permission. Its surroundings support this philosophy, with comfortable furniture, laptop outlets, relaxing music, and a public bathroom; *and* you will find plenty of food and dessert items to keep you sustained all day.

This massively simple and hugely successful approach to adding value yielded Starbucks a level of popularity so strong that the company has become part of our everyday lives. The idea seems so obvious now that you understand how Starbucks does it. But how can you come up with your own simple solutions for maximum impact?

Imagine for a moment that tomorrow morning a new law will go into effect prohibiting you from charging money for the product or service your business sells. How would your company make money? That's easy enough to answer, right? It wouldn't.

But what if you *could* charge for all those little extras you currently just throw in with every purchase? What added value do you provide your customers as a matter of course? There are the obvious freebies, such as free shipping and gifts with purchases. But what about the myriad extras you provide to your customers without even thinking about it, such as appointment reminder cards, newsletters, or even a parking lot? What else could you offer that would add value to your brand in a way that is meaningful to your superniche?

Now that you're thinking about added value, realize that the value does not have to be tangible. It's human nature to first acknowledge the added value that can be seen, heard, touched, and especially quantified. A bar brings in a palm reader on Fridays. A store offers free gift wrapping on all purchases. A customer can listen to satellite radio while on hold.

But what about the intangible ways in which your company provides added value to your customers and clients? Think about experiences, feelings, attitudes, and even the personality of your brand. An accounting firm always starts consultations on time. A sales team is trained to make women feel beautiful when they purchase clothing. A gym has a social, partylike atmosphere.

Sometimes the added value is simply in the way you interact with your marketplace. Perhaps you've trained your staff to smile big, remember customers' names, and compliment customers often, creating a welcoming atmosphere. Or maybe you have designed an environment that is energetic and fun, so that when customers enter your company's space, they feel alive and happy. The feelings that your brand elicits, the state of mind and body that your brand inspires—these are all valuable additions to what you do or sell.

"As soon as I saw your sneakers, I knew I would enjoy the presentation." I hear this all of the time. People know that they're in for a fun ride when they see my jeans and brightly colored sneakers. They know that I've got something different, something *more* to offer than the last person they listened to. Humor is one of the ways I add value to my presentations, and my audience knows it's going to get this value as soon as it sees me—as soon as I *invite the audience members* to join me in my presentation.

An important distinction when identifying added value is that your marketplace doesn't have to know what the added value is; it just has to receive that value.

That bears repeating.

Your marketplace doesn't have to know what the added value is; it just has to receive that value.

There's no need to educate your marketplace about the added value it will receive or has received. The audience members may not be able to articulate what they received, but they know that you provided something extra, something valuable that differentiates you from the pack. Added value must be self-evident. While it's tempting to toot your own horn, especially when the value you provide is amazing and brilliant, you must never force the message down your customers' throats.

You don't have to explain that you offer added value. You just have to do it.

Adding value *is* differentiation. Adding value is one of the most satisfying aspects of my business. This is the step where people get crazy with excitement as they see the wealth of opportunity that is hidden right under their noses. It's a bit like being a kid in a candy store with a pocketful of cash: Oh! I have this value and that value and here's another one and I could do this and then maybe some of that, and so on. Once you get the "adding value" bug, you'll never quit. It's addictive. You'll always be looking for new ways to add value for your customers.

In this step, you will continue to build your brand identity by discovering the ways in which you already offer added value to your marketplace and how you can step up your efforts to provide even more value. You'll explore the difference between a simple extra, like the hairdresser giving his customer a cup of coffee while she waits, and the truly World Famous, market-leading strategies for adding value. Are you ready for a line of customers out the door?

CHAPTER 18

A Problem Is a
Golden Opportunity

"You know, we should punish Polo."

George, my COO at my former company, Propaganda, was suggesting that we punish one of our biggest clients.

"Punish Polo! Why?" I asked.

"Because they just placed two orders that they need within two days again! They know we ask for thirty days advance notice for all orders, yet here they are again, asking for a favor," explained George. "We should make them *wait* thirty days. That will teach them!"

I asked George to take a seat and then closed the door to my office.

"Are you crazy? You want to punish our biggest client?" I exclaimed, standing before him. "You want to piss off the client that pays most of the bills around here? You want to teach a *lesson* to the client that puts food on your table and mine, pays your mortgage and mine, all because its orders don't fit into your schedule? *Are you crazy?*"

Eventually George agreed that punishing our biggest client

was not in our best interest, no matter how tempting the thought. But just as he opened the door to leave my office, he turned and said, "You know, I'm not the only one who wants to punish Polo."

And he was right. At our next staff meeting, I discovered that nearly everyone on our team was frustrated with Polo except me! Polo was in frequent need of favors. Every time Polo needed a favor, I said it was no problem. And every time I said, "No problem," a strain was placed on our entire team. The guys in the warehouse had to work faster and harder. Purchasing had to call in favors to get badly needed merchandise quickly. Accounting had to squeeze out more funds to cover the sudden added expenses. Everyone at Propaganda had to rush to deliver on Polo's request and my promise, and then rush to catch up on other orders. I discovered that there was a general conversation brewing at Propaganda that represented resentment toward our biggest and best client.

I realized that we had a little problem.

At our weekly staff meetings, we made a point of routinely focusing on problem solving, taking the point of view that all problems are in fact opportunities in disguise. Even though we asked our clients to place their orders no less than thirty days prior to the date the goods would be needed, even the most organized, efficient clients still needed a favor from time to time. Requests could change or get overlooked, or sometimes clients would get busy, distracted, and behind, which caused them to order late. It wasn't that Polo was a "bad client" that had to be punished; we just didn't have a system in place to deal with the scenario effectively and profitably.

The solution was not exactly rocket science; it was a rush order service. Since Polo typically rolled out a specific visual branding theme package for several hundred stores over a period of months, and since we would have advance notice of the theme package and how many stores would receive it, we were able to invest $20,000 in extra inventory and prepackage it in anticipation of Polo's rush orders.

For example, if we knew that the winter Polo Sport Package would be going to 150 stores in the quarter, or that the Polo Gentleman's Package would be going to 200 stores in the next few months, we would purchase and prepack core items that would be part of those packages. The prepacked items could be used only for rush orders, so that when Polo called for a favor, it was easy work.

For our new rush order service, we introduced a 20 percent surcharge. Our solution was a huge success with Polo and our other clients.

Let me explain why.

Part of the secret to adding value is the *wow* factor. The *wow* factor must apply to everyone involved, not just the client. We realized that Polo actually felt bad when it had to call in a favor and order late. You could often hear the embarrassment and nervousness in the client's voice when asking for yet another favor, followed by a heartfelt apology. None of our clients felt good about ordering late, which meant that they probably had to summon up their courage to call us. Fear is not the emotion we were hoping to conjure up in our clients!

Yet once *we* were excited about the rush order service, the clients' attitude changed. Once we had a system for handling rush orders, and especially once we had a price for doing so, our whole company actually loved getting rush orders. Because we charged more for rush orders, everyone on our staff benefited via our bonus program. And with our staff happy to take rush orders, our clients no longer felt nervous about calling in a favor.

Once we started charging for rush orders, the perceived value was obvious. Now a rush order was no longer a favor; it was simply a different type of order. The new system took the pressure off both the client and us. Our attitude toward last-minute requests changed. Rush order? Great! *No problem.* The goods were in stock and ready to go, and thanks to our new pricing, our profits were up. A *wow* for the client and a *wow* for us. Do you see how that worked to everyone's advantage?

How did we come up with this fabulous plan? By someone complaining about our biggest client! One of the best, most effective, and most ingenious ways to find added value for your customers is to look closely at your internal complaints. They are a gold mine, and all that is required is that you change the way you look at staff complaints.

Every problem is an opportunity in disguise. When you exorcise those demons—those annoyances; those complaints from your staff about clients; the mistakes; the misconceptions about your customers, your business, and your industry—you come up with brilliant opportunities to *wow* clients and *wow* your own company.

The secret to adding value is in your complaints. Some people ask customers what they want, but I'm a firm believer in the reality that most people often don't know what they want—but they do know exactly what they *don't* want. I never knew I wanted a TiVo, I just knew I hated missing the *Teletubbies.*

Build added value by listening to your complaints and problems and then reverse-engineering solutions, and voilà! You have the doorway to a neverending list of opportunities to add value. Just as Starbucks parlayed complaints from coffee shop regulars into creating a welcoming environment where you can sit all day, just as Empire Carpet identified customer complaints about long waits for flooring consultations and installations and then created a hugely successful business dedicated to same-day installation, you can find the gold mine in your own complaints.

CHAPTER 19

The Bitch Session

Out of frustration can come moments of brilliance, small changes that solve problems and create a *wow* for everyone concerned. This exercise is guaranteed to be fun because you get to express all the frustration or negative feelings you may have about your customers that you normally keep inside.

As you work through the following questions, write down everything that comes to mind, even those ideas that seem silly, or stupid, or obvious. Write down the complaints you feel a bit embarrassed to admit. Get them all out. Don't think about what you're writing; just laugh and have fun with it. Don't judge or second-guess yourself; just bitch away.

Part 1: Bitching About Customers

1. What is your chief complaint about your clients or customers?

2. What are some of your other big complaints about your clients or customers?

3. What are your small complaints about your clients or customers?

4. What dumb things are your clients or customers always asking or doing wrong?

163

5. What mistakes do your clients or customers routinely make?

6. What are the most outrageous demands your clients or customers have?

7. What misconceptions do your clients or customers have about your business?

8. What gets on your nerves the most about your clients or customers?

9. What do you resent about your clients or customers?

10. What question do you never want to hear a client or customer ask again?

11. What do you wish your clients or customers would finally understand, once and for all?

Part 2: Bitching About Your Business and Industry

1. What is your chief complaint about your company?

2. What small complaints do you have about your company?

3. What aspects of your industry as a whole get on your nerves?

4. What do your competitors do that annoys you?

5. What complaints about your business do you hear most from your clients or customers?

6. What general complaints about your industry do you hear from your clients or customers? These are their complaints about your industry as a whole, not about your company.

7. What complaints about your industry do you hear from other people, whether or not they are clients or even spend money in your industry?

8. What negative comments about your industry do you typically hear from your friends and family?

9. If you could change one thing about your industry, what would it be?

10. What embarrasses you most about your industry?

11. What are the biggest misconceptions about your industry as a whole?

12. What do you feel you have to defend or explain the most about your business?

13. What do you feel you have to defend or explain the most about your industry?

14. What kinds of issues do you hear clients or customers talking about that are not necessarily your "fault," yet relate somehow to your business transaction with them?

15. What do your clients or customers lie about most often?

Part 3: Mining the Problems for Opportunities

In your hands, you now have the seeds for some of the most creative work you may ever take on. You now have the ability to add meaningful value for your clients or customers and increase your level of contentment with and excitement about your own business. All of that translates into increased profits—and, of course, a World Famous brand you can be proud of.

Now take the complaints from both of your bitch sessions and prioritize them based on various factors. You'll need several sheets of blank paper for this task.

1. First, go through the list and identify the complaints that you would *not* change. Before you make this decision, make sure you know why you wouldn't change them (i.e., how the complaint is actually a benefit to your business or your customer). List all the complaints you would not change on a separate sheet of paper and set it aside.

2. Looking at both lists, how would your business be different if you addressed all the remaining complaints? What would your business look and feel like if each complaint were transformed into a *wow* for both your business and your marketplace? How would your business be different from other businesses in your industry if you successfully addressed each complaint on your lists?

3. Now take a look at the remaining complaints on both lists. Without spending much time on it, do you notice a complaint that must be dealt with immediately, one that is *the* most im-

portant complaint of all? If so, skip to Step 7 and then come back to the other steps once you're finished.

4. Next, identify the complaints that bother you the most. Write down the complaints that really get you riled up, in order of importance. The goal is to have a complete, prioritized list of complaints that you do want to fix, with the chief complaints at the top and the least important complaints at the bottom.

5. Using a fresh piece of paper, start a new list of complaints prioritized by the ease of fixing them. Which problems can be transformed into opportunities with the least amount of effort? Place those complaints that can be fixed easily at the top of the list, and those that would require a huge effort at the bottom of the list.

6. Now, take the two prioritized lists and compare them. Do you have any complaints that are in the top 10 on both lists? What about the top 20? What you want is a list of complaints that you have prioritized as both important and easy to fix.

7. Using a fresh piece of paper, write down the complaint that you want to deal with first. This could be one that stood out initially, or it could be one that made the top 10 on both prioritized lists. Just as we developed a rush order policy and fee as a solution to my staff's complaints about Polo's last-minute requests, how could you fix this problem so that it is both a *wow* for your customers or clients and a *wow* for your company? Brainstorm ideas until you come to view this complaint as a golden opportunity, a hidden gem that could boldly differentiate your brand identity from other businesses in your industry.

8. On the same sheet of paper, outline a general plan for implementing the solution to your chief complaint. Remember, this complaint is one that is both important and easy to fix, so the plan should not be complicated or time-intensive.

9. Identify the steps you can take today to implement the plan for your solution. Stop right now and complete these immediate steps so that your plan is set in motion. Each day, complete any and all steps you can in order to successfully incorporate your solution into your business.

10. Repeat this process with every complaint on your list, starting with those that are both important and easy to fix. Work on adding value daily until you have turned every last problem into an opportunity to *wow* your company and *wow* your marketplace.

Using your complaints as fuel for new ideas is both courageous and wise. Facing the truth about your business and your customers allows you to grow as a person and your company to develop into a World Famous brand. Rather than drown in a sea of negativity, you will now look forward to hearing yourself complain again. Our complaints are the simple expression of a problem, and say it with me now: *All problems are opportunities in disguise.* Therefore, complaints equal opportunity when approached from an entrepreneurial perspective.

Just think about all of the coffee shop owners who must have complained about the customers who would buy a "measly cup of coffee" and then expect to sit there all day, taking up space and never ordering anything else. Boy, did they miss the boat! Starbucks figured it out, and while everyone else was scratching their heads and wondering how this new coffee chain could charge such a high price for a cup of coffee, the market basked in the wonderful added value of being able to hang out guilt-free at umpteen locations all over town.

You now have the power to truly differentiate your brand identity by adding mountains of value to your business. You don't have to guess at what your superniche wants; you know what it wants and needs based on its complaints *and* your own complaints about the people in your superniche.

Mining your complaints and problems for opportunities garners the type of added value that makes other businesses think, "Why didn't we think of that?" And when you perceive your complaints and problems as little gems of opportunity, your attitude changes. Each day is spent inventing brilliant solutions rather than cleaning up messes and popping aspirin for that eternal migraine. Business becomes more fun and rewarding. What could be better than that?

Adding Value

Building on the work you have done in defining your superniche and your three-word persona, adding value to your product or service and to your business as a whole is the next step in differentiating your brand. There's a good chance that you already provide added value to your customers or clients in myriad ways. The little extras you provide without a second thought all provide added value that makes an unforgettable impact on your marketplace.

Added value encompasses every aspect of your business, including the intangible ways in which you provide that "something extra" to your marketplace. It could be a feeling, an attitude, or even a smile. Added value does not have to be quantified to count, and some of the most meaningful ways to add value cannot be measured at all.

The way in which you invite your superniche to do business with you is an added value. A high-quality invitation grounded in authenticity establishes an expectation of added value that draws your marketplace in. It signals to the members of your superniche that you have something different to offer that will satisfy their desires and eliminate their frustrations.

The only goal in providing added value is to give it freely. There is no need to explain to your customers or clients that they are receiving added value. Your marketplace doesn't have to know what the added value is in order to get it. Actions speak louder than words and have more of an emotional impact on your customer base.

Every problem is an opportunity in disguise. An effective way to discover new ways to add value to your brand is to pay attention to your complaints—and those made by your staff or colleagues— about your clients or customers. Rather than simply bitch about your least favorite consumers, let the complaint be a clue to a void in your business that, when filled, could provide added value that would result in a *wow* for both your business and your marketplace.

Next, get ready to use your brand profile to engage your marketplace effectively and claim your status as a World Famous brand.*

---

*Download your free brand profile document at www.WorldFamousCompany.com, press the Brand Profile tab, and enter code WF001.

STEP

5

Ready, Set, Engage!

In 1986, John Yokomaya was in deep. After 20 years, his fish market in Seattle's Pike Place Market was about to go under. In a last-ditch attempt to save his business, Yokomaya sought help from a friend's husband, Jim Bergquist, a business coach with innovative ideas and an inspiring message.

During the coaching process, one of the fishmongers suggested that the fish market should become "world famous." Actually, the fishmongers' goal was even bigger than that: They wanted to be "world famous in a way that makes a profound difference for people." This was a tall order, considering the fact that this fish market could not be distinguished from the numerous other fish markets in Pike Place Market. Still, the idea stuck, and Bergquist helped Yokomaya and his fishmongers develop and realize their vision.

Today, that fledgling little fish stand is known as the World Famous Pike Place Fish Market. It's the main attraction at Pike Place Market; customers crowd around the fish market, excited about doing business with it. Customers who can't order fish in person visit the market's web site to watch the live-action web cam and then order fish online. Beyond selling fish, Bergquist and Yokomaya founded a consulting and training company based on their strategies and experiences that focuses on helping corporations empower their employees and realize their own visions—and yes, they toss fish at the corporate trainings, too!

Featured in movies, talk shows, and news programs and in magazines and newspapers all over the world, this company achieved its goal and created a World Famous business. And it hasn't spent one penny on advertising. Not one penny.

How did the company do it? If you've visited the fish market at Pike Place or have seen video footage of it, you know that the people there throw fish. The fishmongers toss the fish to each other and to the customers, and even encourage customers to get in on the action and toss a fish. But is that all? Did the market become World Famous just because of a fish-tossing gimmick?

The answer is no. And really, the fish tossing is not a gimmick at all. It's about having fun and engaging the marketplace in a unique way. It makes you feel great about doing business with the market. It puts a smile on your face and makes you feel as though you are the most important customer in the world. The fishmongers are having a great time—all the time—and it's infectious. You, the customer, want to be part of it, over and over again.

Here is what the World Famous Pike Place Fish Market has to say about engaging its customers (from its web site):

> *We interact with people with a strong intention to make a difference for them. We want to give each person the experience of having been served and appreciated, whether they buy fish or not. We love them.*

We *love* them.

The fishmongers love their customers. They want to offer them an unforgettable, positive experience. They engaged their customers. *That's* how they did it.

This is how a company that at the start was identical to the competition was able to break free from competing at all and stand out as the only choice. If a small, nearly broke fish market can become World Famous, your business can too. If a group of fishmongers can engage its market like rock stars, so can you. And you are now totally prepared to do so.

Like the World Famous Pike Place Fish Market, you have worked hard to develop your brand identity. Just as it dared to become World Famous, you have also dared to stand out from the crowd, to create a powerful vision for your business, infusing your business with vitality and energy.

In Step 2, you zeroed in on your market by defining your superniche. In considering the characteristics of the customers you enjoy working with, you liberated your business from trying to satisfy everyone, enabling you to focus all of your resources on people and businesses that truly appreciate what you do. You discovered the psychographic of your demographic, the aspirations, frustrations, and values of your superniche—a powerful tool in creating a brand identity that resonates in the hearts and minds of your customers.

Just as the World Famous Pike Place Fish Market differentiated its fish market from *every other fish market in the world*, you differentiated your business. Just as the fish market determined that it was actually in the entertainment business, you discovered the true industry in which your business operates. This shift of focus allowed you to develop the personality and attitude of your brand and describe that personality using three powerful, essential, earthshattering words. Just as the fish market used the words "World Famous," your three-word persona became the foundation of your brand.

As you continued to build your brand identity, you identified the world that your customers could live in vicariously just by doing business with you. And you developed the promise of your brand, just as the fishmongers decided that their promise was to make a difference in the lives of their customers.

In Step 4, you mined your frustrations and complaints to find ways to add value for your customers. Just as the fishmongers go out of their way to make their customers feel comfortable by happily answering their questions about fish and seafood—even going so far as to provide them with recipes and cooking tips—you figured out how to up your game and offer a uniquely satisfying buying experience for your customers.

Your hard work has paid off. You now know your brand inside and out. You possess a top-of-mind awareness of your brand. Your knowledge is a secret source from which you can draw any answer about your brand identity. Using this source, you can determine how to approach every aspect of branding and marketing your business. You can cut through the noise of too many tactics and options and hone in on the right path for your business. Armed with your secret source, you will not throw money away on ineffective marketing and advertising.

You now have a failure-proof way of getting to the hearts and minds of your customers—and staying there.

You are ready.

In the fifth and final step, you'll examine all the ways in which your business touches the world and how each one of these is part

of your brand identity. You'll learn the concept of business ergonomics, or how you can make doing business with your company a
pain-free, pleasant experience for your customers. You'll identify
the areas of your business that may cause customers to zone out
and how to change them, and you'll learn the "rules of engagement," simple filters to help you ensure that you are engaging your
marketing authentically and in keeping with your brand identity.

But first, let's put your brand profile together into a working
document. You've come a long way. Stop and appreciate how far
you've come, and recognize the powerful tool you have created in
your World Famous brand profile.* It's time to toss your own fish. I
dare you.

---

*Download your free brand profile document at www.WorldFamousCompany.com,
press the Brand Profile tab, and enter code WF001.

CHAPTER 20

Exercise—Putting It All Together

Before you get down to business, I want to tell you about my friend Roberta. Not long before we moved to Hawaii, we were vacationing on Oahu, and we decided to take a drive out on the coast road toward the North Shore. As the end of the day approached, we went in search of a great place to watch the sunset and have a cocktail. We came across a town called Punaluu, and there we found a quaint-looking pub not far from the shoreline. It looked promising, so we pulled off the road and parked the car.

I will never forget the first time I walked in the door of the East Shore Bar. Right away I felt uncomfortable. Several patrons turned and stared at us, as did the bartender, a large-framed, shaved-head hulk of a man. I wondered if this was a biker bar, or worse. I didn't know if I wanted to stay or run like hell.

With no host to greet us, I felt uncertain as to what to do and where to sit. The restaurant had plenty of tables and chairs, but they were all empty, so we weren't sure if we were allowed to sit there. Yet the bar was positioned way in the corner, about 30 feet in the back, as if in a separate space altogether. And even though there were only a handful of people in the place, every bar stool was taken.

Was I supposed to seat myself? Was I supposed to walk 30 feet to the bar and announce my arrival, even though I knew that everyone knew I was there? Did the East Shore Bar offer table service? How did this place work? Did they want me there? Was I going to get beaten up?

With the sun setting fast and not wanting to look stupid, I persevered and looked around. The bar was a sprawling, ramshackle, worn-out joint with mismatched plastic and wooden chairs and plastic tablecloths on the tables. An assortment of wobbling, antiquated fans spun from various points in the ceiling, and an ancient rear-projection television sat across from the bar, with old boxes, folding chairs, and other junk piled up behind it.

Just as I was thinking that we should move on and find somewhere more fitting for our sunset cocktail, the bartender asked if we needed any help. Good question, I thought. Again the patrons turned on their stools and stared. Not wanting to look like an uptight yuppie, I immediately ordered two mai tais. Two people made room for us at the bar, and we sat down.

Before I knew it, we were in conversation with the bartender, and, as it turned out, Scott was very friendly. Soon we were talking with several of the locals at the bar, and everyone was so welcoming that I felt silly for all of my apprehension and rush to judgment.

After our second drink, a woman named Roberta came in and sat down next to me. She was the owner of the bar, and in the course of our chatting, I learned that she had purchased the place on a whim just a year before, trying to fulfill one of her lifelong dreams of living in paradise. Roberta and I talked and talked and talked. It got to the point where I was regretting that we had to drive back to our hotel, which was a good 40 minutes away. When we got up to leave, Roberta, my new best friend, offered us a guest room in her house on the beach just down the road.

It took us about three seconds to make up our minds, and we graciously accepted. I liked Roberta and felt like I'd known her for a long time. We ended up staying an entire week, during which time we spent many evenings at Roberta's bar. Over the course of that first week, I had many conversations with Roberta, and not surprisingly learned that her business was not going as well as she had hoped. Roberta was frustrated, to say the least.

During our week at Roberta's, I noticed that every single day numerous people came to that same front door and then turned around and left. I also noticed that those who timidly stayed were not comfortable. One evening I asked Roberta how *she* had felt the very first time she walked through the door, before she owned the bar. She told me in detail just how intimidated she had felt and how rude the bartender and patrons had been. I started laughing and told her that as a thank-you for her generous hospitality, my gift was to consult with her on my return to Hawaii.

When we moved to Hawaii in 2005, Roberta insisted that we stay with her for the first few nights, so our consulting sessions began almost immediately. We developed the personality traits of her business and discussed the attitude she wanted her bar to present. We discussed psychographics at length, how she wanted her patrons to feel, and what kind of attitude she wanted to generate in their hearts and minds when they arrived at her bar or even just *thought about* her bar. Again, the theme was along the lines of *Coyote Ugly* meets Hawaii. It was all about leaving your troubles at the door and being in a place where you could be yourself, a place where you could let your hair down and have a good time. As we refined our work, we chose words such as *escape, freedom,* and *uncomplicated.*

With her brand profile complete, decision making became easy, and Roberta went to town overhauling her business. She became totally enthralled by it. Suddenly issues that had once burdened her became easy to resolve. Roberta now knew exactly what kind of establishment she was running. She knew its personality and its attitude, and that knowledge gave her power. It became both a call to action and an acid test for all of her planning.

Roberta had a big sign made that sat at the bar entrance. In the shape of a surfboard, the sign read, "No Shirt, No Shoes, NO PROBLEM!" She also had other signs made that reflected the carefree attitude of her bar. She worked on the ergonomics of her business, changing the layout of the entrance so that it would be more inviting and instructing staff on how to greet customers.

Roberta even reorganized the menu, making it simpler and more profitable, and introducing menu selections and cocktail descriptions that brought the carefree attitude of the place to life. The menu was a large, nicely designed sheet that included fun slogans, a story about the bar, and directions on how to relax and have fun there. A loaf of bread with a big chunky carving knife was delivered to each table. Roberta even started drawing up plans to expand the bar area so that it wasn't such a walk from the entrance.

After a few months, Roberta came to visit me in Honolulu. Sporting a new outfit (and a new Louis Vuitton bag), she looked excited and happy. She insisted on treating us to dinner at the ritzy Longi's Restaurant overlooking the Pacific Ocean. Over champagne, she announced that she had had her best two quarters ever. More importantly, she loved running her business and finally felt that *she knew what she was doing*.

That's Roberta's story. How will your story play out?

Exercise: Putting It All Together

Since you already have all the pieces of your brand profile, you may have already combined them into one document. If you haven't, do so now. Take a look at the amazing result of your hard, creative work. Does the brand profile you've created make you feel more confident? Do you feel armed and ready to engage your marketplace in a meaningful way? Are you certain that you are now prepared to chart a course for your brand that will ultimately result in World Famous status?

I hope you answered yes to all those questions. If not, don't worry. I'm not going to send you back to repeat an exercise. It's natural to have some fear about moving forward. As you stare at the piece of paper that holds the key to your World Famous brand, the road ahead can seem daunting. You might even freeze up and have to set the paper aside for a few days until it all sinks in. You may need to read it over and over again to make sure you got it right. All of this is okay. Revel in the success that is a completed, winning brand profile that, when utilized, will definitely change your life forever.

Exercise: The Story of Your Brand

I have one more task for you, one more inspiring exercise that will help you to clarify your purpose and manifest your destiny. I want you to write the story of your business. Using Roberta's story as a guide, write your own story from the beginning to the future that lies ahead. Here are your guidelines:

1. First, write the beginning. How and when did your business start? What inspired you to start your business? What were your initial aspirations for your business? What did you do to ensure that your business got off to a good start?

2. Next, write the middle of your story, which is what your business was like just before you decided to pick up this book. Were you happy with the state of your business? Were you successful? Were you making money? Did you feel fulfilled professionally? Describe everything you can about your business, both good and bad.

3. Now, write the ending yet to come. Roberta's story had a happy ending thanks to the work that she put into building her brand. What end result do you hope to accomplish with this process, and how will you achieve it? What is the ultimate destiny you want this brand-building process to help you meet? What steps will you take to ensure that your brand becomes World Famous, by whatever standards you deem appropriate?

Your story does not have to be perfect, or even grammatically correct. Just pour your heart out and be as descriptive as possible. As you move forward engaging your marketplace, it's important that you keep both your brand profile and the story of your brand in mind at all times.

I want to congratulate you for completing all the exercises up to this point. This is no small feat, and I hope you feel proud of this accomplishment. It's time to get on with it and reap what you've sown.

CHAPTER 21

Engaging Experiences

"I want all my senses engaged. Let me absorb the world's variety and uniqueness."

—DR. MAYA ANGELOU

People buy experiences. Knowing this puts you ahead of the game. Utilizing this knowledge gives you an almost unbeatable edge over the gazillion other companies offering similar products and services.

Recall that in Step 2, you learned that people make purchases based on the story of their lives. Utilizing that knowledge helped you to define your superniche based on the psychographic of your demographic. When you fine-tune that vital marketing secret further, it is clear that people buy *experiences* that fit into the story of their lives.

As a consumer, you already know this to be true. When you shop, you choose the companies that offer you the best package of experiences, such as proximity to your home, price, and customer service. Or you may be choosing one specific experience over all other factors, such as the return policy, the size of the dressing room, or the expert knowledge of the staff. You automatically gravitate toward businesses that can provide the experience you want to have and what it will feel like when you shop for and eventually buy something, unaware that you are making decisions based on how you want to feel.

This applies to spur-of-the-moment purchasing decisions as well. Mom and Dad are tired after schlepping around the mall all day, and the kids are hungry. Will they choose a family-friendly restaurant in the mall or pack up the family and head to a different restaurant across town? At that moment, Mom and Dad are most likely looking for something fast and uncomplicated where kids are welcome. The mall restaurant becomes the only choice because it can provide the experience that fits into the story of Mom and Dad's life at that moment. Is it any surprise that most eating establishments in malls are geared toward families?

It's not just about the experience of having; it's also about the experience of purchasing. This is why it is so important that you learn to engage your superniche effectively, resonating with its members on an emotional level so that they see your business as the only choice for getting the experience they want to have.

How do you create compelling experiences for your superniche? First, you have to know how your marketplace wants to feel, which you've got down cold. Second, you've got to have personality, baby. And you've got that. You even have three words to describe the exact personality and attitude of your brand, which means that you can create a positive experience for your consumers that is both unique and authentic to your brand.

From a quick look around at other businesses in your marketplace, it's clear that many companies aren't thinking about how they want their superniche to feel—heck, they probably don't even *have* a superniche. But even if they do have a well-defined target market, it's still a safe bet that most of the businesses in your industry are not concerned with the experience they are providing to their customers. So again, utilizing this knowledge gives you an *unbeatable edge* over the competition, so much so that you are the only choice. Can't beat that now, can you?

From now on, whenever you think about your product or service, think about it as an experience that you are offering to your superniche. The experience begins the first time a prospective customer hears about your business. From then on, the experience of doing business with you, even if it is just a thought that he *might* do business with you, lives on in the heart and mind of each customer. There is no end. A relationship has begun, and you are responsible for nurturing that relationship. With this responsibility comes the ability to shape and steer that relationship. *That* is a huge gift, and it deserves your gratitude and steadfast commitment to providing authentic experiences for your customers.

In order to succeed, you must consistently deliver experiences that engage and inspire the people in your superniche while they are in the process of doing business with you. This requires that you look at every aspect of your business and where it touches the world—which will be addressed in the following chapter.

Engaging your market effectively also requires that you pay attention to the multisensory aspect of doing business with your company: sight, sound, touch, smell, and even taste. Take Disneyland, for example. The theme park is not only filled with fantasy characters and buildings, but also is impeccably clean and beautifully landscaped. No matter where you go in Disneyland, you will hear lovely music, whether it's live or playing from a loudspeaker. At Disneyland, patrons are able to touch their favorite Disney characters, play interactive games, and, of course, fondle endless souvenirs.

Despite the masses of people, Disneyland still smells of flowers and yummy treats. Which brings me to taste. Around every corner, you will find new wonders to taste that will delight you. It's a multisensory *experience* that leaves patrons feeling totally satisfied. Disneyland even has water misters located throughout the theme park that blow mist every so often to cool off patrons in scorching hot weather!

Engaging your superniche also requires looking at the whole picture. Zoom out until you can see the beginning, middle, and end of your engagement with the marketplace—not an end to the relationship, but the end of one specific engagement. If it helps to think of this as one transaction, go with that terminology, but remember that the beginning is the moment when a customer first hears or sees something about your business, *not* the first time she contacts you or enters your establishment.

Jay Leno, host of *The Tonight Show* on NBC, provides us with a great example of how to engage the marketplace uniquely. *The*

Tonight Show is a huge profit center for NBC. In fact, the show is such a big success that Jay Leno's most recent contract was $100 million. (Conan O'Brien takes over for Jay in 2009 and has some big boots to fill.)

Part of the appeal of *The Tonight Show* is the live audience. Leno plays off his audience from the moment he steps on stage until the credits roll. This energy has to be big in order to carry through the television into millions of bedrooms and living rooms, but somehow it does. How does *The Tonight Show* pull this off five nights a week? Let me tell you what happens when you go to a live taping of the show.

It's the big day. You're excited because, let's face it, you had to jump through a few hoops to get tickets. When you arrive at the studio in Burbank, you wait in line for a while, and then, 30 minutes before showtime, you are greeted by staff members from the show, who walk you into the studio and help you find your seat. There's electricity in the air. Technicians are working on the set, and you can see the famous desk you've watched on television all these years. The studio is bright and exciting, and you are filled with anticipation.

Before you have a chance to get antsy, the stage manager comes out from backstage and welcomes you. The mere sight of her with her headset and clipboard makes you feel special, as if you have been let into an exclusive club.

"Ladies and gentleman, welcome!"

The audience is so excited that it gives the stage manager a round of applause. Caught up in the moment, you join in too.

"My goodness, what a good-looking audience we have tonight. Far better looking than yesterday's crowd!"

You laugh. The audience laughs. Already it's funny, and the show hasn't even started yet.

"Who here would like to be part of a history-making show? We want to make this show the absolutely best *Tonight Show ever*, but we can't do it without your help. So let's run through some guidelines. Anyone interested?"

More applause. Everyone, including you, is totally into this experience. You feel even more important now; you even sit a little taller in your seat.

"Great! Now, if we're going to work together and make this the best show ever, we have to get to know each other. Please, ladies and gentlemen, introduce yourself to at least five people you have never met and welcome them to *The Tonight Show.*"

The audience is buzzing. People are shaking hands and smiling. You meet five people who seem to be just as happy as you are, practically bubbling over with excitement.

"Okay, now that we're old friends, let's give ourselves a big round of applause!" The audience applauds, but the stage manager does not seem satisfied.

"I thought you wanted this to be the best show ever! What on earth was that? Even last night's not-so-good-looking audience did better than *that.* Let's try again. And just to make things easier, here's the applause sign."

Just then a big sign that reads, "APPLAUSE," lights up in red. Everyone applauds much louder.

"Fantastic! Now sometimes things happen on the show that are *really* funny, so when you see this big red light start spinning *and* the applause light blinking, guess what we want you to do?"

With the applause sign blinking and the red light spinning, the audience erupts in applause and cheers. You notice a giant clock on the wall that seems to be counting down to showtime. This puts you on the edge of your seat.

A comedian comes out to entertain you while you wait. He's funny, and you're having a great time. Every few minutes he reminds you of how much time is left, and now you're practically bursting at the seams.

"Only one minute until it's *your turn* to be part of the best *Tonight Show ever* . . . and three, two, one . . ."

Music. An announcer. And then Jay Leno appears. The crowd goes crazy, and you are right along with them, clapping and cheering. As Leno delivers his opening monologue, you are pumped and ready to laugh, applaud, and cheer. You are totally engaged in what he is saying, and you stay engaged throughout the show because you feel like a key component of the show. You're going to make history, after all!

How would *The Tonight Show* come across if the audience had been stuck waiting outside for hours, with no shelter from inclement weather, no access to a bathroom, and no information from the show's staff as to what was happening next? Would the show be different if the audience was ushered in like cattle, had to push aside candy wrappers and empty Coke bottles to find a seat, and had only seconds to settle down before Jay Leno himself walked out on stage? What kind of a reception would he get from his audience if its members were uncomfortable, hurried, nervous, frustrated, or (worst of all) bored? How would his guests feel if the audience had no clue as to how to respond to their witty stories and every joke fell flat? How would the show come off on television if the audience were disgruntled and confused?

The experience of watching *The Tonight Show*, whether you do it from the studio audience or from the comfort of your own home, must make you feel engaged. How many businesses do you know that take the time to engage their audience, their market, so that it is ready for what is about to be offered? How much time do you currently take to get your audience, your superniche, in the mood to do business with you?

Armed with the secret that people buy experiences coupled with your vast knowledge of your brand, you can now look at each aspect of your business with the goal of creating experiences that will inspire your superniche to do business with you.

C H A P T E R   2 2

Touch the World

Imagine that your business is a fried egg.

I'm serious.

I know it sounds silly, but just go with me for a minute. In the fried egg that is your business, the yolk is what you do or sell, such as Polo Ralph Lauren's clothing and home décor and Virgin Atlantic's air transportation. Now imagine the pan in which the egg is being fried. That pan represents the marketplace, your audience. I just call it "the world."

Now look at the egg white. Wow. The egg white sits between what you do or sell and the whole wide world. Do you have any idea what the egg white represents? This isn't a test; I ask just to illustrate that in business, most people believe that in order to succeed, they need to work harder, focusing on the yolk (what they do or sell) and the pan (the world, or getting customers). It's all yolk, yolk, yolk and pan, pan, pan. They overlook the egg white while concentrating all of their resources on the yolk and the pan. Yet the egg white is a powerful space. It's what *connects* their business (what they do or sell) to the world.

In the fried egg analogy, the egg white represents opportunity, because it is where your business touches the world. It is where you engage your marketplace.

The space that is the egg white is where you reflect the industry in which your business operates, express the personality and attitude of your business, and communicate the vicarious world—the playground—that your business represents. The egg white is where you create your relationship with the world, engaging your marketplace in a meaningful way that resonates in the hearts and minds of your superniche.

Stimulate or bore, attract or repel—all is possible within the egg white. It's entirely up to you what happens in this space. Magic can happen in the egg white. It can make your business World Famous. Even if your yolk happens to be an iPod or a pair of Jimmy Choo shoes, you still have to focus on the egg white because it is where your marketplace *experiences* your brand.

When you look at all of the places your business touches the world, how many of them can you say make a real impact? In how many places do you grab people's attention and make them feel fantastic about having a relationship with your business?

Look again. How many of your business connections are just mediocre? In how many ways have you inadvertently chosen to fit in and do things just the way everyone else does? How many aspects of your business could be approached in a unique way so that when they do touch the world, they make an immediate and lasting impact?

I guarantee that even now, as you think about all of the areas where your business touches the world—your egg white—you are not fully aware of at least half of them. Everything is significant, even your own name. Look at Ralph Lauren, born Ralph Lifshitz. With the vision that this Bronx-born entrepreneur had for his life and his business, is it any wonder that he changed his name? He knew his birth name did not evoke a *feeling* of prestige, wealth, or finer things. But the name "Ralph Lauren" could inspire masses of people to believe that the man behind the brand really lived the good life that his clothing represented.

In the next exercise, you'll discover all the ways in which your business touches the world so that you do not miss one single opportunity to engage your marketplace in a unique way.

Exercise: Fry Your Egg

On a large piece of paper, draw a fried egg. Make sure the egg white space is large enough to allow you to write lots of notes. In the yolk, write down the name of your business and what you do or sell. Outside of the fried egg write, "The world/my market." This exercise is all about the egg white, so you are done with the yolk and the pan.

Remember, the egg white represents opportunity.

Within the egg white, write down all the different ways in which your business touches the world. List every way in which your company comes in contact with your marketplace. I even include the piece of plastic that surrounds my car license plate. Why should it advertise the auto dealer when it could present my business in some way? Here's a short sample list to help you jump-start your brainstorming:

- ✧ E-mail
- ✧ Snail mail
- ✧ Web site
- ✧ Telephone
- ✧ Voicemail messages
- ✧ Advertising
- ✧ Invoices
- ✧ Printed media
- ✧ Waiting rooms

Now look at each item and break it down into its separate components. List every detail that pertains to contacts with customers or clients and with the marketplace at large. For example, if you use e-mail, then list e-mail, e-mail signature, and e-mail subject line. Or for printed media, you might list business cards, brochures, flyers, holiday cards, thank-you cards, letterhead, envelopes, mailing labels, applications, and surveys.

Breaking each item down helps you to see other possibilities, to have clever realizations that can really give you a more accurate picture of how you connect to your marketplace. So now I want you to go back and brainstorm for other ways in which your business touches the world. This time, try to think outside of the box. How do your customers find out about you? How do they first have contact with you? What are the steps they take to do business with you? Here's another short sample list to help you continue to brainstorm:

- ✧ Meetings
- ✧ Member organizations
- ✧ Charity events
- ✧ Sponsorships
- ✧ Trade shows
- ✧ Press/media
- ✧ Online forums
- ✧ Referrals from customers
- ✧ Referrals from other businesses
- ✧ Packaging
- ✧ Flyers
- ✧ Brochures
- ✧ Business cards
- ✧ Shopping bags
- ✧ Shipping boxes
- ✧ Signage
- ✧ Promotional videos
- ✧ YouTube-style videos
- ✧ Product design
- ✧ P.R. news
- ✧ Books
- ✧ E-books
- ✧ Corporate gifts
- ✧ Thank-you cards

- ✧ Your clothing
- ✧ Speeches
- ✧ Elevator pitches
- ✧ Networking
- ✧ Promotional events
- ✧ Your vehicles
- ✧ Other people's vehicles

Once a man on eBay offered to tattoo a logo on his forehead for the right price. The list of places where you might touch the world never ends.

What you're going for is a detailed, comprehensive list of all of the ways in which your business comes in contact with the world, which is your marketplace. The list may never be complete, as there are always new ways to touch the world. But with this list, you now have a picture of the myriad ways in which you do indeed have contact with your marketplace. Going forward, your mission is to apply your brand personality to each one of these areas with the intention of engaging your marketplace. You're out to inspire people to do business with you, so you need to put your personality, your stamp onto each one of these areas. Each item on your list is an opportunity to engage and inspire your market. That's one powerful to-do list!

Gone are the days of nondescript business cards, boring voicemails, lackluster customer service, and dull advertising. From now on, it's *not* business as usual, it's business as *you*.

Dare to be genuine, to stand out from the crowd and fully express the personality and attitude of your brand. Let each aspect of your business that touches the world sing with the playground and promise of your brand.

Remember, this is not about showing off or drawing attention to your business just for the sake of doing so. This is about putting your authentic brand persona to work for you.

As you go down the list of ways in which your business touches the world, use the same filters you used to rank active words in your three-word exercise: mediocrity, excitement, and call to action.

Let's use e-mail signatures as an example, because everyone uses e-mail and everyone should have an e-mail signature that engages his marketplace.

In applying your brand personality (your three-word persona) to your e-mail signature, you would use the filter of mediocrity to ensure that your engagement strategy is not similar to or the same as that of your competitors and other businesses in your industry. The next filter is easy: Does your new e-mail signature excite you? Does it thrill you every time you see it? If not, go try again. The third filter asks you to determine whether your e-mail signature is a call to action. What does it ask your marketplace to do? If the answer is "nothing," you need to modify your e-mail signature until there is a clear call to action that engages your marketplace.

In Chapter 25, you will learn the rules of engagement, which will also help you make sure that your brand personality is applied consistently and powerfully.

Even if you operate a simple, one-person business, the list of ways in which your business touches the world could be very long. It's way too much to bite off in one sitting. Make a commitment to apply your brand personality to at least one area on your list each day until you have made it through your list. The first few days will take longer than the last, so take heart. It seems like a mountain of a task now, but small steps really add up. And if you feel inspired, tackle more than one area in one day. Go for it. When you're on a roll, keep at it, and soon every aspect of your business will be in line with your authentic—and hard-earned, I might add—brand identity.

Choose the areas around your fried egg where you see you can have the biggest effect on your market, and focus on applying your brand identity to those areas first.

On your list of places where your brand touches the world, where are you possibly being mediocre? Where are you falling in line with other companies and not staying true to your brand? Focus on those areas too, as you can have a big impact on your superniche when you can turn a typical "zone-out zone" into a place where you are engaging your market uniquely.

CHAPTER 23

Business Ergonomics

How many businesses do you know that intimidate you? How many stores make you feel uncomfortable from the moment you walk through the door? How many businesses alienate you *at the mere thought* of having to pick up the phone and call them? Everyone has a list of businesses that she would rather not revisit. Short or long, this list is made up of businesses that have given no thought to business ergonomics.

Perhaps you are just bored waiting in line for what seems to be an eternity. Maybe your back hurts from the waiting room chairs. Maybe the voicemail system cut you off before you could leave a message. Perhaps you are frustrated by the amount of paperwork you have to fill out *every time* you come in.

The negative or frustrating experiences you have had with other businesses show you the result of nonexistent business ergonomics, and yet you may not have given much thought to the ergonomics of your own business. Sure, you put out fires as they come up, and you do your best to keep your customers or clients happy. But have you really taken the time to evaluate your business systems to discern whether they are consistent and provide maximum efficiency?

Business ergonomics is about ensuring that your systems are

seamless, engaging, and consistent with your brand identity statement. The last thing you want to do is insult, irritate, frustrate, or alienate the people in your superniche, especially from the get-go. When your systems require excessive and unnecessary steps, they create discomfort and fatigue for your clients or customers. Even minor annoyances can be a turn-off for the people in your marketplace and make it impossible for you to win them back. And those customers that *have* to come back to you in order to complete a transaction or because you are the only local option do so grudgingly, which means that they are not fans of your brand and can damage your brand through negative word of mouth.

Many business owners just accept delays and hiccups as par for the course, and so do not spend any time refining their systems so that these things don't happen again. Over time, the seemingly random problems become part of doing business, and rather than improve the system, business owners accept them and work around them. With this attitude, all you'll end up with is a business that is known for having a chronic problem and being unable to address it. Yet when you work to provide a seamless, effortless experience for your customers or clients, eliminating any stress associated with doing business with you, you gain a loyal fan base and positive word of mouth.

Most business owners are caught up in day-to-day operations and so haven't thought much about being truly engaging. Even if their systems function well, they often don't implement those systems in a way that excites their superniche and genuinely represents their brand personality. They get the job done, people generally seem pleased with their business, so what more is there to do? Plenty.

You didn't pick up this book and work so hard building your brand in order to create a mediocre business with a lukewarm following. You want a World Famous brand, and engaging your market in a *systematic* way will help you get it. To achieve business ergonomics that delights your clients or customers, you need to provide engaging experiences at every stage of doing business with you. No task is too small, no area unworthy of your attention.

As I mentioned earlier, business ergonomics is also about consistency across all systems. People often assume that consistency is just about having business cards that match the letterhead and the invoice. It is so much more than that. What I'm talking about here is consistency with the personality and attitude of your business. Every single element of your business must reflect your three-word persona and the vicarious playground and promise of your brand. By "everything" I mean *everything!* Your printed material and web site, of course, but also the layout of your waiting and meeting rooms, your customer service, your sales campaign and marketing, the flow of the space, the signs on the back and front door, even the way you run your employee-only back office.

To recap, business ergonomics requires seamless, engaging, consistent systems in all aspects of your business. Imagine a chiropractor's office. What items do you usually see in the waiting room? Chairs, small tables, some old magazines, and maybe a plant? What if, instead of asking people to sit in hard chairs reading magazines, the chiropractor engaged them in the world of health? Imagine that same waiting room with mats to stretch out on, a small library of health and wellness reference books, toys and books for children, refreshments, and sublimely comfortable massage chairs? Wouldn't this be a fantastic, meaningful, rock-star way for this chiropractor to achieve business ergonomics? I know that if I experienced that waiting room, I would have a better experience all around and would never miss an appointment.

To inspire your marketplace, think about streamlining your business systems and aligning them with your brand identity statement. What you're going for is maximum comfort and ease for your superniche, which means that the ergonomics must also fit the psychographic of your superniche. Remember, people buy experiences, and the experiences they want are those that fit the story of their lives. Create a harmonious, seamless experience for your customers or clients that engages them in an exciting way and your World Famous brand is as good as done.

Exercise: I Spy Ergonomics

At the beginning of the chapter, you explored the businesses that turn you off because the business ergonomics is off or nonexistent.

Take a few minutes now to think about one or two of your *most* favorite businesses and identify the ergonomics of those businesses. For example, if you love the sushi place down the street, think about the last time you went for dinner and sake. What was it about that experience that made you love it so much and want to come back again soon? Perhaps the restaurant welcomes you by name, seats you immediately, and has chairs that are just the right size. Maybe your sushi spot prepares the food quickly and beautifully, and there's not a bad spot in the restaurant. Perhaps it is a cool hole-in-the-wall spot with unique graffiti on the walls that have been added over time by satisfied patrons. Keep an eye out for what other companies do that makes *you* want to go back.

Identifying the systems of the businesses that you enjoy and frequent will help you to identify the systems in your own business that are working well and those that could be improved.

Exercise: Ergonomics and the Fried Egg

Look at your lists from the exercise in the previous chapter, and take each of the ways in which your business touches the world on an ergonomic test drive. Remember, business ergonomics must be seamless, engaging, and consistent with your brand identity statement. Make notes of the areas that are hitting the mark on all counts and those that need to be modified.

Exercise: The Walk-Through

I'm amazed how many business owners have no idea what it's like to be one of their clients or customers. One of the best ways to see how the ergonomics of your business is working (or lacking) is to do a walk-through of your business as if you were a client or customer. Start by trying to find a business that offers the product or service you sell. So, if you're in the organic home industry disguised as a nontoxic dry cleaning business, let your fingers do the walking and try to find *your business*. What's it like to look for a business like yours?

Next, call up and pretend to be someone in need of answers or assistance. Create a problem or customer service issue and see how your staff resolves it. Ask about policies and price to get a feeling of how people experience your business for the first time.

If you can pull it off, walk into your own business and pretend to be a customer. Not everyone can walk into his own business unnoticed. So, adopt a disguise and have some fun with it. If that's not your bag, ask one of your friends to do it for you and report back to you. Give her a few specific things to look for so that you can receive a detailed report.

Personal shoppers make their living from evaluating businesses based on the specific criteria that you set forth. Some will perform the task in exchange for the merchandise or service that they procure in the process, and others also require an hourly or per-project fee. There are agencies that will set this up for you, and this may be required if you have a large business with multiple locations. But if you have one business or one primary way for people to experience your business, I would recommend meeting with your personal shopper in person so that you can get exactly what you want from the experience.

Of course, you can also glean a lot from simply taking a walk through your business and imagining what it would be like to be one of your customers or clients. The experience of doing business with your company must be seamless, consistent, and engaging from start to finish. Do any or all of these things until you have an accurate picture of the experience that your business provides.

If you are a Web-based business, visit your web site as if you were a potential customer landing on your home page for the very first time. Imagine that you don't know how to navigate the site, and try to find what you're looking for. Or, ask someone who has not been to your web site to do a virtual walk-through.

CHAPTER 24

Zone-Out Zones

We were late for the convention, and I was stressed out. The Las Vegas Convention Center was at the absolute end of the strip from our hotel, a good 15-minute drive. Fully prepared to stew and fret for the entire ride to the convention, I was surprised to see a karaoke machine and two microphones in the backseat of the cab. We were in a karaoke cab! Cruising down the Las Vegas strip, I belted out songs like "Margaritaville" and "Crazy Little Thing Called Love." All of my stress evaporated on the second verse of the first song, and I completely forgot about being late for the convention.

The cabbie was really fun and totally into the experience, despite the fact that he had probably heard dozens of people sing that day. When we arrived at the convention center, I gave him a great tip, and then, before I got out of the cab, I asked him why he had a karaoke machine in his cab.

"Most cabbies complain about their customers and complain *to* their customers, but I have a great time with them," he said. "And, I live really well in a big house. I make more than most of the people who ride in my cab."

If one guy in a cab can make ten times as much in tips by engaging his marketplace, you can do the same with your business. What the karaoke cabbie did was up the ante and change the experience so that we were no longer simply exchanging cash for a ride, we were laughing and singing and having a fantastic time. The karaoke cabbie elevated the experience so that the normal exchange of money no longer applied, and I felt compelled to give him a tip worthy of that experience, worthy of taking me out of my grumpy mood and delivering me at my destination happy and energized.

The backseat of a cab is the perfect example of a place that usually qualifies as a "zone-out zone." Zone-out zones are areas or ways in which your business is experienced that cause your marketplace to zone out. In other words, they are the aspects of your business where you are most likely to lose your customers or clients. Zone-out zones represent mediocrity. Customers are lost because they are bored—or, rather, because *you are boring*.

Everyone wants to be engaged. If people are not engaged, no longer tuned in to the present moment, they zone out and start thinking about other things. I wonder who will get voted off the island tonight. Should I take out some chicken for dinner, or just order in? What on earth is she wearing? How come I always stand in the slow line? Why *did* Britney shave her head?

Remember, you want the people in your superniche to be totally engaged from the moment they come into contact with your brand until the transaction comes to an end. In order to accomplish this, you need to identify the zone-out zones of your business systems and replace them with engaging experiences. In the rest of this chapter and the next, you'll explore the top offenders, the most common zone-out zones, and how you can elevate those experiences so that they are completely engaging.

Voicemail Messages

Remember when you recorded your first voicemail or answering machine message? The novelty of it usually resulted in some seriously wacky, creative messages as you tried to one-up your friends. Of course, it was just for personal use, and you probably graduated to boring personal voicemail messages eventually—whatever gets the job done and gets you on your way. But there was something about those inventive, silly messages that made your friends call your number just so that their date could hear how clever it was.

Back then, you wanted to be different, and you hoped that your message would stand out in your crowd. You need to return to this level of excitement and creativity when you record the voice-mail and hold messages for your business. You need to think outside of the proverbial box and come up with a message that once again engages your superniche, because frankly, your customers and clients are zoning out in a major way. No doubt about it. And by now you know that *any* zone-out zone is bad for business.

How many times have you tried to bypass a voicemail so that you could leave a message and get on with your day? How many voicemails do you actually remember (aside from those early gems that you and your crazy pals created)? When was the last time a voicemail inspired you to do business with the company you were calling? On the flip side, how many times have you been either put off or totally *uninspired* by a voicemail and so chose not to leave a message and called another company instead?

I advise my clients and seminar participants to create a new voicemail as their first act of engaging their superniche because it is something that everybody can do, and it doesn't cost a dime. You don't need to hire anyone to do it for you, it won't take forever to implement, and you will notice immediate results. Also, other than the Internet, your voicemail message is the first contact you will have with your marketplace. You cannot overestimate the importance of an engaging voicemail.

If you need help creating a fantastic voicemail that is in keeping with your brand identity, visit my web site at www.World FamousCompany.com.

CHAPTER 25

The Rules of Engagement

Recently I rode in an elevator with several flight attendants from Virgin America, Richard Branson's brand-new airline for the American market. They were staying at my hotel, and when I noticed their uniforms, I told them how much I loved flying Virgin Atlantic. A few complimentary words from me, and they were off, extolling the virtues and innovations of Virgin America.

The flight attendants told me how much they loved working for Virgin and how the experience was far superior to that at every airline they had worked for in the past. They simply loved working for Virgin, and they knew exactly what the brand stood for. When the elevator stopped at their floor, they didn't want to stop talking. They wanted to keep talking about the brand, *their brand*, because they were genuinely excited about the experience.

It was an all-out love fest, and it shows what can happen when a World Famous brand engages its marketplace effectively. Every aspect of Virgin America's business is geared toward engaging its superniche in accordance with the personality, playground, and promise of the brand, including the enthusiastic flight attendants who want to tell everyone they meet about their fun and unique company.

The process of engaging your own superniche can seem overwhelming, especially when you look at the fried egg that is your business and consider all the ways in which your business touches the world. What you need are rules of engagement, parameters that help you keep on task and on point.

You will get results when you start applying your brand identity to your business, and when you commit to being uniquely differentiated. The more you dare yourself to stand out and be authentic, the better the result.

What follows are my guidelines, my rules for engaging your marketplace effectively. The rules will help you stay grounded as you implement your World Famous brand profile, and help you determine if your strategy is successful.

Rule 1: It Must Engage

This seems obvious, but even after reading an entire chapter about engaging your marketplace, the obvious is often overlooked in favor of complicated and "clever" strategies. Often people approach branding without really thinking about what it's for. They want to be "cool" or "hip" or just "get on with it" so that they can get down to business.

There's only one reason to have a brand, and that is to inspire the marketplace. So when you talk about engaging, remember that it is all about inspiring your superniche to do business with you.

Rule 2: Know Your Brand Beforehand

You've already done a lot of work toward building a solid, World Famous brand profile. But the work of knowing your brand identity is really never done. Your company will grow and change in order to meet the demands of your superniche and rise to the challenges and advances in your industry.

Rule 2 is about knowing your brand identity before you commit to any changes in your business or your brand. While you may be tempted to hire a graphic designer or another consultant right off the bat, it's important that you know exactly who you are before you welcome any outside opinions.

I recommend hiring experts when it comes to design, and when your brand profile is firmly ingrained in you, you can ensure that the results are in keeping with your goals and your brand identity statement. I've seen it happen time and time again. A company that has no idea of what it wants or who it is hires a graphic designer, hoping that the designer will help define the company. The end result is something that is neither powerful nor inspiring, and that may actually turn off the company's superniche. When you approach a graphic designer or Web designer with a carefully created brand identity, you ensure that your logo, graphics, and web site fall in line with your brand. Test it out. Give your designer a copy of your brand profile and see what he comes up with. You will be amazed. Even just telling a prospective designer your three words will give him a clear understanding of your brand identity.

When you are clear about what you are looking to accomplish in the design aspect of your business, you will end up with business collateral that clearly represents your three-word persona, the vicarious playground of your brand, and the promise of your brand.

Rule 3: Your Mother Doesn't Have to Like It

You can't please everybody, and you shouldn't even try. The only opinions that matter when it comes to your brand are yours, those of your colleagues and/or staff, and that of your superniche. Unless Mom is a key person in your company, don't ask her what she thinks of any aspect of your business. The same goes for your wife or husband, your girlfriend or boyfriend, and your best friends. In fact, I always know it's a good sign when my Mom's response to my work is, "I don't like that." Do you know what I tell her? "Good. You're not supposed to like it."

It may sound harsh, but my Mom is not my market. If your close friends and family do not fit the demographics and psychographics of your superniche, don't worry about their opinion. All that is important is that you stimulate your superniche. End of story.

Rule 4: Repetition Is Key

Repetition is about delivering consistency and not giving up on your strategies. If your engagement plan doesn't create the exact results you had hoped for right from the start, don't give up. As long as you are receiving a positive response and your plan is in alignment with your brand identity statement, you're good. Too often, people give up on their dreams and their goals because things don't pan out right away. Yet it can take several attempts to reach the hearts and minds of your superniche. People need repetition in order to remember your business, especially in today's multitasking, option-crazy, 24/7 society.

Likewise, changing tactics too soon in order to get a better result just confuses your superniche and diverts its attention. When you are consistent in your approach, and that approach is consistent with your brand identity statement, it's only a matter of time before your brand compels your superniche to do business with you.

Remember on *Seinfeld*, how every time someone said something shocking, Elaine would say, "No way!" and push that person? People always laugh at this, in part because they know it's coming. The more Elaine does it, the more laughs she gets. This is the beauty of consistent repetition. Your superniche is conditioned to *anticipate* the experience your brand is providing, which means that it expects this experience *and* wants it.

Consistent repetition also means that you spend less time engaging your market, because you don't have to reinvent the wheel. For example, my clients expect a witty voicemail message from me. They would be shocked if I suddenly recorded a boring message. Boring is not consistent with my brand.

Rule 5: You Can Afford to Be Larger Than Life—*Authentically*

Despite the long list of ways in which your business touches the world, your superniche does not come into contact with your business as much as you do. In general, your customers or clients are in touch with your business no more than once a day, whereas you are living your business every minute of every day. This is why you can afford to be larger than life.

Your fear of standing out, of drawing attention to yourself, is so pervasive and intense that it will come up time and time again as you build your World Famous brand. The fear that you are "over-doing" it may be a tempting excuse to tone down your efforts to engage your marketplace, but you won't overdo it. You can't. Your superniche is not going to think your efforts are "too much" because it isn't really spending much time doing business with you. And your customers won't get bored with the repetition either, for the same reason.

Dare to go big, to be larger than life. Your World Famous brand depends on it.

Ready, Set, Engage!

With your brand profile now complete, you have a comprehensive knowledge about your brand identity that is priceless. This knowledge is also all you need in order to engage your marketplace brilliantly. You are absolutely ready to launch your very own World Famous brand.

With top-of-mind brand awareness, you can confidently make decisions about every aspect of marketing your business. Every dollar you spend on branding and marketing will produce fantastic results *because* you have done the hard work of building a World Famous brand. *And,* you will not be wasting your time considering myriad options that aren't congruous with your brand identity. In building your brand profile, you have truly created a powerful asset and an eminently useful tool that will reap dividends exponentially.

People buy experiences that fit the story of their lives. World Famous brands provide engaging experiences at every stage of their relationship with consumers. It's not just about the experience of owning a product or partaking of a service; it is also about the experience of *purchasing* that product or service.

Your superniche craves an engaging experience, and you can easily provide that by stimulating its psychographic. Remember that you considered the psychographic of your superniche in the development of your three-word persona, brand playground, and brand promise. Those three elements that make up your brand identity statement fit the people in your superniche perfectly, and so you have a head start in creating experiences that engage these people effectively, even dynamically.

Do you see the vital knowledge that you have acquired? It's even more amazing when you realize that the vast majority of businesses do not possess this knowledge. Most businesses are clueless about branding, and even fewer businesses know that people buy engaging experiences that fit the story of their lives. The advantage is yours. You are heads and tails above the pack. You are well on your way to becoming the only choice in the hearts and minds of your marketplace.

Engaging your superniche should be a multisensory experience, providing brand-congruent stimulation for all five senses—sight, sound, touch, taste, and smell—wherever possible. Effective engagement also involves considering the beginning, middle, and end of transactions with consumers. Are there any steps that need to be ramped up in order to engage your superniche?

I like to use a fried egg as an example of how your business touches the world, where the yolk of the egg is what you do or sell, the pan is your marketplace, and the egg white is where your business touches the world, where you *engage* your marketplace.

Within the egg white are myriad ways in which your business comes into contact with your marketplace, everything from advertising to business cards to your web site. Magic can happen within the egg white because each aspect of your business presents an opportunity to communicate your brand identity and cultivate a relationship with your superniche.

Use the fried egg analogy as a tool to discover all the ways in which your business touches the world, and then apply your brand personality to each of them. You don't have to do anything drastic. Even small changes can help you engage your marketplace as long as those changes come from a place of authenticity and are congruent with your brand identity. It's not about getting attention for the sake of getting attention; it's about putting your brand identity to work for you.

When you consider all the ways in which your business comes

into contact with your marketplace, you must ensure that each of them is ergonomically correct, or in alignment with the psychographic of your superniche. Business ergonomics is providing experiences for your customers or clients that are seamless, engaging, and consistent with your brand identity statement. Nonexistent business ergonomics inspires frustration and discontent as your clients or customers attempt to work around the obstacles and issues that you have (knowingly or unknowingly) set up for them in order to do business with your company.

World Famous brands engage their superniche using ergonomically correct systems that provide the utmost comfort and inspire brand loyalty. From start to finish, their customers or clients are completely engaged in the experience of doing business with them. This is the goal. And again, just *knowing* the goal and the path to get there puts you leaps and bounds ahead of other businesses in your industry.

There are some aspects of business in which companies are often indistinguishable from others, areas where people accept sameness and a boring attitude as par for the course. These areas are zone-out zones, where your customers or clients *disengage* with your business and "zone out." When you inspire your superniche to tune out and think of *anything other than your business,* you have lost an important opportunity to resonate with it in a meaningful way. You may even lose its business entirely.

Part of engaging your marketplace brilliantly is eliminating zone-out zones by transforming them into engaging experiences. One of the best ways to experiment with this is with your voicemail message, which is one of those zone-out zones where "boring" is considered perfectly acceptable. This is one of the best ways to begin engaging your marketplace because it's free, it takes very little time to implement, and you can see an immediate result.

Your voicemail message is of primary importance because it is often the first contact your prospective customers or clients have with your business. Another first-contact aspect of your business that is almost always a zone-out zone is your waiting room or reception area. Again, it's easy to fall into the trap of doing what other businesses do and failing to see how asking your customers or clients to *wait to do business with you* in a boring, irritating room is actually harming your brand.

By their function, waiting rooms are designed to frustrate your marketplace. But what if that same space was used to *prepare* your marketplace to do business with you? What if the function of the room was to get people warmed up to your brand? What if you could actually monetize your waiting room, so that it was one of your biggest money-making assets? You'll be amazed at how simply changing your perspective on the function of the space inspires innovative ideas that will truly set your business apart.

Creating a preparation room that is in keeping with your brand identity statement and business ergonomics is a huge step toward engaging your marketplace brilliantly. Remember, most businesses throw some matching office furniture, factory-made art, a few plants, and some magazines into the space and forget about it. By revamping the space where clients or customers usually wait to see you, you are creating an engaging experience that compels people to do *more* business earning you *new* money.

As you implement your plan to engage your marketplace, there are five rules that will help you stay focused and on track.

1. *It must engage.* The *only* goal is to inspire your superniche to do business with you. Period.

2. *Know your brand beforehand.* Before you commit to working with experts and making changes to your business, be sure that you know your brand inside and out and can communicate your brand identity statement with ease.

3. *Your mother doesn't have to like it.* The opinions of the people in your superniche are the only ones that matter. Don't get caught in the trap of trying to please everybody in your business and personal life.

4. *Repetition is key.* Consistent repetition of your efforts to engage your superniche makes your brand memorable and reliable and allows you to avoid reinventing the wheel each time you set out to connect with your marketplace.

5. *You can afford to be larger than life.* Because your customers or clients do not come into contact with your business as often

as you do, you can afford to be larger than life in your approach.

Now that you know how to engage your marketplace, your business—and your life—will never be the same. In fact, if you follow the strategies outlined in this book, it will surpass your wildest dreams.

Exercise: Let's Party!

To celebrate your massive accomplishments, I want to prove to you that you are ready to launch your very own World Famous brand. To do that, you're going to plan a party. This is not just any old party. This is your Brand Identity Party, the big celebration announcing your arrival. It is also an exercise to help you see your brand profile in action and practice engaging your marketplace.

Of course, you can throw an *actual* party anytime you want; you certainly don't have to throw a big bash if you don't feel confident that you have created a truly World Famous brand—yet. However, I urge you to plan the launch (or relaunch) party now, even if you would rather wait until you're 100 percent ready. It's a fantastic exercise that will show you how much you've accomplished and help you gain confidence about your new brand identity.

As you answer the following questions, be sure to have your brand profile handy to refer to and keep your brand identity statement firmly in your mind. Have fun!

1. Would your party have a theme, and if so, what would that theme be?
2. What season and time of day would you throw this party?
3. What would the invitations look like? How would they be delivered?
4. Who would be invited to your party? Would you have VIP guests, and if so, would they be treated differently?
5. Describe the ideal venue for your party.
6. What kind of food and drinks would you serve?

7. What type of music would be playing? Would you hire a band, a soloist, a DJ, or a strolling guitar player?

8. Besides music, what type of entertainment would you provide for your guests?

9. How would you expect your guests to dress?

10. Would you hire people to staff the party, and if so, in which roles? How would the party staff be dressed?

11. Describe the décor of the event. What is the primary color palette? Is it refined and sophisticated, wacky and wild, or something altogether different?

12. What kind of experiences are people having? Are they dancing? Networking? Singing karaoke? What kinds of activities or games are you planning for your party, if any?

13. What is the general mood of your party? Are people laughing and letting their hair down? Are they exchanging business ideas?

14. What is your role at the party?

15. Do you have a big announcement to share, or a speech to give? If so, describe your intention. What about recognitions, presentations, ceremonies, or awards?

16. How do you want your guests to feel during the party? What do you hope they will feel and believe about your brand after the party? What actions do you want them to take during and after the party?

17. How will you follow up with your guests after the party?

Your brand profile provides all the information you need to answer these questions. Isn't it cool how that works? Since you utilized your brand profile and the strategies you have learned in this book, your party will be distinctive and feel authentic. You'll never have a run-of-the-mill party again. Your party will be unique and will have your name all over it. It will be legendary. Famous. World Famous. Just like everything your company does from this moment on.

Onward!

I was running late. Like a true pro (and faithful Englishman), I had topped off several long days attending the Magic Show in Las Vegas—the largest men's retail trade show in the world—by staying out late with clients. So not only was I late for the airport, I was hung over. I felt awful, and I wanted to get home. As I snaked my way through the lobby of the Las Vegas Hilton, I noticed a sea of people waiting for taxis.

I was irritated, but I had no choice but to wait in line with the hordes of hotel guests. As I stood in line, I entered my own personal zone-out zone; my mind wandered to random thoughts, totally disengaged.

"I wish I hadn't had those last 16 drinks last night," I thought. "I wish I had an Alka-Seltzer."

As I got closer to the door, I noticed a commotion in the line. People were standing on tiptoe and nudging each other. Some of them were smiling. I had no idea what was going on, but it piqued my interest.

Finally I could see what all the fuss was about. Everyone's attention was fixed on a hotel employee opening taxi doors for guests. People were mesmerized, engaged in the door opener's shtick. He was a pleasure to watch, and he had something clever or funny to say to everyone.

He approached an elderly couple, obviously married for an eternity, who were next in line for a taxi.

"What a *beautiful* daughter you have, sir," he declared cheekily, clearly referring to the man's wife as he beckoned the couple toward their cab.

They beamed and gave him a tip. After the door closed, the door opener held a $20 bill in the air and said very loudly, "Thank you!"

It was hard to tell if he had actually received a $20 tip from the couple, or from anyone else. But no matter how much he received, he still held up a $20 bill for all of us to see.

Next in line was a gaggle of teenage girls. "Oh my goodness, we have to get you out of here," he exclaimed, rushing them into a taxi. "What happens in Vegas stays in Vegas!"

The girls giggled and gave him a tip. Again, he held up a $20 bill and said loudly so that everyone could hear, "Thank you!"

No more zone-out zone for me. I was totally engaged in what was going on. I wondered what he would say about me. Everyone around me strained to watch, exchanging knowing smirks with each other. They were smiling and laughing and wondering what he might say to them when they got to the front of the line. No longer bored or frustrated, the crowd was enjoying the experience—of waiting!

"I'd better suck it in a bit," I joked to the people around me. I had this feeling that I was about to be on stage. I was excited because I was about to have the full attention of this guy, and of everyone else.

I decided that I was *not* going to give him $20. What could he possibly say that would make me give him more than $1 or $2—I'm English! I don't tip $20!

Finally, I made it to the front of the line, a bit nervous, wondering what would happen. The taxi door opener screamed when he saw me.

"Brad Pitt!"

I gave him the $20.

When I got home, I did some research. I learned that the average taxi door opener in Las Vegas makes about $45,000 a year. Would you be surprised to learn that *this* Las Vegas Hilton taxi door opener makes $450,000 a year? That's not a typo. A taxi door opener makes nearly half a million dollars a year, which, as I'm sure you've figured out by now, is almost all tips from happy hotel guests. He doesn't make 50 percent more than other taxicab door openers, not three or four times more, but *ten times* as much as a typical taxi door opener in Las Vegas.

This isn't Apple. This isn't Starbucks. This is a guy who is actually providing a *free service*. The $20 tip he gets paid for opening doors is because he was engaging. He caught our attention and took us out of our zone-out zone. He inspired us. He did every single thing that this book says.

The Las Vegas Hilton taxi door opener chose his place in the market, rather than let the market dictate his place—or his income. He dared to think outside the box, zeroed in on his superniche, and differentiated his brand by defining his industry and creating a brand personality, playground, and promise. Daring to stand out, he engaged his marketplace by providing an experience from start to finish, so that even the people in line are compelled to do business with him. Remember, for the taxi door opener, this means that he must compel people to *give him money for a free service*!

Does the taxi door opener know his marketplace? Yes. And by holding up the $20 bill, he shows the suggested retail price for his services. Some people don't tip, but he acts as if everybody does. Is this guy adding value? You bet he is—he called me Brad Pitt! In fact, I'm going so far as to say that he's throwing the door opening in for free. When you engage your market uniquely, you get paid what you deserve.

Anyone can do this. This happened years ago, and I'm still talking about him. You can compel your marketplace to do business with you. You can inspire brand loyalty and cultivate raving fans. You can get your marketplace so excited about doing business with you that it will move heaven and earth to do so.

You don't have to be Apple. You don't have to be Starbucks. You don't have to be Joe Boxer, Ralph Lauren, Virgin Atlantic, or any of the other World Famous brands you studied in this book. You just have to be you. Authentically you.

Here's to your World Famous brand. I look forward to hearing about your amazing success. Now, go forth and inspire your marketplace!

Index

Index

Index

Index

Index

waiting rooms, 209

walk-through, business ergonomics and, 196–197

Wall Street Journal, 12

Wal-Mart, superniche market of, 38–39, 61

Walton, Sam, 38

web site, personality of business and, 87

Wilman, Andy, 94

Winfrey, Oprah, 58–60, 101

World Famous Pike Place Fish Market, 172–175

wow factor, 161–162

Yokomaya, John, 172–175

zone-out-zones, 192, 198–200, 208